AD Non Fiction
799.2973 P842r

Posewitz, Jim. Rifle in hand : how wild America was saved   9001145117

DISCARDED BY
MEAD PUBLIC LIBRARY

MEAD
PUBLIC LIBRARY

Donated by Jim Baumgart in honor of conservationist, author and Sheboygan native Jim Posewitz

RIFLE IN HAND
How Wild America Was Saved

Jim Posewitz

RIVERBEND
PUBLISHING

Copyright © 2004 by Jim Posewitz

Published by Riverbend Publishing, Helena, Montana.

Printed in the United States of America.

1 2 3 4 5 6 7 8 9 0 CH 10 09 08 07 06 05 04

All rights reserved. No part of this book may be reproduced, stored, or transmitted in any form or by any means without the prior permission of the publisher, except for brief excerpts for reviews.

Cover and text design by Laurie "Gigette" Gould.
Illustrations by Jim Stevens.

ISBN 1-931832-45-5

Cataloging-in-Publication data is on file at the Library of Congress.

Riverbend Publishing
P.O. Box 5833
Helena, MT 59604
Toll-free 1-866-787-2363
www.riverbendpublishing.com

The American Hunting Trilogy
Rifle in Hand is the third volume in a series of books on American hunting by Jim Posewitz. The other titles are *Beyond Fair Chase* and *Inherit the Hunt*. For more information on these titles, please contact Riverbend Publishing.

"To think straight on recreational quality, an historical perspective is essential."

ALDO LEOPOLD
"WILDERNESS VALUES," *THE LIVING WILDERNESS*, 1942

Dedication

This book is dedicated to Sarah Catherine, daughter of Matt and Heather Posewitz. Sarah is the family's first born of her generation. The dedication extends to any siblings or cousins that might occur as her generation finds its way in the 21st Century. It is my hope that the hunt, and the desire to engage in fair chase, will be carried forward in the traditions of North American families. We know how the wildness that remains on this continent was rescued and delivered to Sarah and her generation. We also know that aging hunters carry a responsibility to pass the wild estate forward so another generation may savor a rare privilege—the chance to be a hunter.

This dedication also extends to the thousands of hunter educators throughout the United States and Canada. These volunteer instructors prepare more than a half-million hunters each year. They teach the new hunters to be safe, to hunt responsibly, and to embrace the heritage that is theirs. There is no way to thank them enough.

ACKNOWLEDGEMENTS

Thanks to David Stalling, Chris Cauble, and Laurie 'Gigette' Gould for editorial, design, and organizational support of this effort as it worked its way to completion. Appreciation for early encouragement and technical assistance is extended to my friend Johnny Stowe and to Linda Renshaw, both of the South Carolina Department of Natural Resources. An early review by Kevin Lackey was most helpful. Hunter education coordinators from various states provided fact verification, perspective, and encouragement—in particular, many thanks to Eric Nuse of the International Hunter Education Association, Lenny Rees of Utah, Rod Slings of Iowa, Helen McCracken of Wyoming, and Pat Dorscy of Colorado.

Critical review and valuable comments were graciously offered by Professor John Reiger of Ohio University Chillicothe; John Organ, U.S. Fish and Wildlife Service; Father Theodore Vitali, Saint Louis University; Dr. Valerius Geist, University of Calgary (retired); and, Christopher 'Kip' Koss. Mr. Koss is Jay Norwood Darling's grandson and executive director of the foundation, faithfully nurturing "D'ing's" legacy. My brother John did most of the digging to reveal the family history, and his wife Mary provided hospitality and shelter, all being greatly appreciated.

Finally, special thanks to Montana wildlife biologist Gayle Joslin for her support, encouragement, critical review, and above all, for her companionship through this and other projects.

While all of these people provided valuable assistance, the author retains full responsibility for both the concepts and details expressed in the telling of this story.

Contents

Foreword 9
Introduction 17
The Train from Lithuania 23
Last of the Buffalo Hunters 29
The Conservation Idea 37
Taking Action 46
The Great Occasions 55
Taft, Peril and Posterity 77
The Hunt That Must Survive 89
Preparing the Future 95
Epilogue 103

THE COVER ART

"In the Mountains" depicting Theodore Roosevelt was painted by Montana cowboy artist Charlie Russell in 1905 and is in the permanent collection of the Montana Historical Society in Helena, Montana. Colonel Wallis Huidekoper, a "Rough Rider" under Roosevelt during the Spanish American War, originally owned the painting. It is not known whether the painting is a representation of an actual event or a reflection of stories that Russell had heard. TR made numerous hunting trips into Montana and did kill a number of grizzlies during his time in the west. When Russell made this painting, Roosevelt was President of the United States. Special thanks are given to the Montana Historical Society and its Curator of Art, Kirby Lambert.

Protection of grizzly bears in Montana began in 1913 with the creation by the state legislature of the Sun River Game Preserve, which later became part of the Bob Marshall Wilderness. In 1923 the protection and management of grizzly bears was guaranteed when the state classified them as game animals. The "great bear" was never absent from Montana and was expanding its occupied range when the 21st Century began.

Foreword

Primeval Connections

America's hunting and wildlife heritage teeters on a precarious perch. There are those who would lead us towards a more European model of animal husbandry and privileged hunting in which hunted wildlife are treated as a commodity, artificially manipulated to produce large-antlered animals for the highest bidders to shoot. Others defend our hard-won, uniquely American system. It is a system in which wildlife belongs to all, is managed as a public trust with equal opportunities for all Americans, and which fuels the conservation, protection, and enhancement of wildlife and the wild places that sustain them.

There's no doubt where Jim Posewitz stands. Since retiring in 1993 from a distinguished 32-year career as a biologist with the Montana Department of Fish, Wildlife and Parks, Jim has been a fierce, untiring advocate of America's distinct wildlife and hunting heritage—showing us where we came from, where we've gone astray, and what we need to do to get back on track.

His first book, *Beyond Fair Chase: The Ethic and Tradition of Hunting*, has become the bible on proper and ethical conduct for hunters, influencing thousands of young hunters in hunter education classes across the Continent. His next book, *Inherit the Hunt: A Journey Into the Heart of*

Hunting, delves even deeper into the history of North America's hunting and wildlife heritage, its democratic roots, and the growing, dire threats of privatization and commercialization of wildlife and hunting.

"This hunting tradition and the conservation ethic within that tradition covered a lot of ground before it got to us," Jim wrote in *Inherit the Hunt*. "This legacy did not come to our generation to die. To keep it alive, we must learn the stories, we must appreciate their significance, and we must teach each successive generation how this heritage was delivered into our custody."

Here, in Jim's latest book, are some of those stories, significant stories, stories that all of us who hunt and care about wildlife should read and learn and pass on to others. In Jim's words, "Stories that helped me understand the value of hunting in America." Through his stories, Jim takes us along on a notable journey of recurrent, important connections to George Perkins Marsh, Theodore Roosevelt, Aldo Leopold, Jay "D'ing" Darling and many others. More importantly, he shows us that we *all* have such connections, we all have similar stories—we're all part of this remarkable legacy.

Until I met Jim Posewitz, I never paid much attention to such connections. Like how I spent a childhood, and then some, chasing striped bass along the shores and islands of the Connecticut coast—just a short boat ride away from where, in 1842, a common oysterman helped define the public ownership of wildlife in America; or how I grew up in the same state where, in 1896, there initiated a Supreme Court case firmly establishing the notion of wildlife being held "as a trust for the benefit of all people." I developed a love for wildness playing in tidal estuaries just down the coast from estuaries where Theodore Roosevelt once roamed and developed his notable fondness for wild things. Like Aldo Leopold, I studied forestry and moved West. Like Roosevelt, I developed a passion for chasing wild elk through truly wild country and became, like him, a wilderness hunter. Like Roosevelt and Leopold and George Perkins Marsh and Alfred Aldrich Richardson and Jay "D'ing" Darling and Jim Posewitz . . . and hundreds and thousands of other hunters through the course of our Nation's history, all across North America, my desire to conserve wildlife and wild places, my conservation ethic, derived from appreciation gained through arduous pursuit of fish and game. Jim sums it up nicely: "Hunting was the passion driving the people who committed themselves to the task."

Like Jim, "I took to the hunt because somewhere within my nature throbbed the rhythm of the chase. . . . To satisfy the urge I wandered wild places. . . . I killed and savored the gift of wild things." And in the countless hours and miles of unpredictable adventure chasing magnificent creatures such as stripers and elk and deer, I've come to deeply cherish the animals and the places they roam. Kindled by the chase, my devotion to wildlife sparked my concern for their well being and their habitat.

These are the primeval connections that bind our heritage—vital connections between predator and prey, between wild things and humans, between conservationists past and present. We abandon these connections at our peril; we *must* come to understand and nurture this heritage because, as Jim says, "What we understand, we can honor and sustain."

Perhaps the most valuable lesson I've come to understand from Jim is the crucial importance of the arduous pursuit—the "doctrine of the strenuous life," as Roosevelt put it, "skill and patience, and the capacity to endure fatigue and exposure, must be shown by the successful hunter." Unfortunately, there is an ongoing quest to make hunting easier, quicker, with more sure-fire results, changing the fundamental relationship between predator and prey. A look through most any hunting equipment catalog shows a plethora of technology available to the modern hunter, including trail-monitoring devices to photograph, record, and store animal movements, game scanners, hearing enhancers, night-vision goggles, range finders, animal scents, ATVs with gun mounts, and thousands of other gadgets designed to increase our chances of finding and killing wildlife. Several years ago, hunters in northern Idaho were shooting elk from a half-mile away using .50-caliber rifles mounted on off-road vehicles. A game warden from Wyoming tells me that every year, more and more hunters use airplanes to locate elk, radioing their sightings to friends on the ground. Some so-called hunters simply pay to kill fenced, domesticated big game animals on game farms. In Texas, hunters commonly lure deer into automated bait stations and then shoot them from luxurious towers.

When hunters seek easier ways, focusing only on results and skipping the process (or, as Roosevelt put it, those who are "content to buy what they have not the skill to get by their own exertions"), they fail to gain the intimacy, knowledge, appreciation, and respect for the prey, for the habitat, and for other wildlife that is gained through arduous pursuit. The connections are shattered. I suspect this growing disconnect is, in large part, why some hunters are either apathetic or outright opposed to policies that protect and enhance wildlife and wild places; they either ignore, or never really came to understand, our hunting and wildlife heritage.

Several years ago, over a beer or two, I shared with Jim

a story of frustration. While working to protect wild places, some fellow wilderness advocates chastised me for being a hunter. At the same time, some fellow hunters derided me for advocating wilderness. "I don't feel a part of either group," I told Jim, "I just don't know where I fit in." He laughed. "You know why?" he asked, smiling, leaning in close as if to let me in on some great secret. "Because you and I, we're Leopoldians, and there aren't many of us around."

Of course, he might just as well have said "Rooseveltians," or even "Posewitzians." Thanks, in large part, to Jim's persistent efforts (and efforts of the organization he founded, *Orion—The Hunters Institute*) there are, everyday, more and more of us Leopoldians around.

In his 1949 classic, *A Sand County Almanac*, Aldo Leopold wrote:

> I have the impression that the American sportsman is puzzled; he doesn't understand what is happening to him. Bigger and better gadgets are good for industry, so why not for outdoor recreation? It has not dawned on him that outdoor recreations are essentially primitive, atavistic; that their value is contrast-value; that excessive mechanization destroys contrasts by moving the factory to the woods or to the marsh. The sportsman has no leaders to tell him what is wrong. The sporting press no longer represents sport; it has turned billboard for the gadgeteer. Wildlife administrators are too busy producing something to shoot at to worry much about the cultural value of the shooting.

Fortunately, Jim Posewitz has emerged as a leader— gently telling us what is wrong, wisely showing us how to get back on track, helping us understand where we've been and where we need to go.

This book is packed with wonderful stories of our past, present and future; here's a short one of my own:

In the fall of 1999, my friend Bill Hanlon was hunting Dall sheep with two of his friends in the spectacularly wild 2.5-million acre Tatshenshini Wilderness of northwest British Columbia. Six days into their hunt, walking along the face of a 20-foot wall of ice, they found the 550-year-old, well-preserved remains of a human hunter, recently exposed on a receding glacier, replete with a knife-like tool called a tugwat and an atlatl, an ancient hunting tool used to hurl spears into prey. The body was recovered by the Champagne and Aishihik First Nations, who dubbed the man *Kwaday Dan Sinchi*, or "long ago person found." Researchers say the person was male, in his 20s, and most likely fell into a crevasse and died. The country he once hunted and died in is probably not much different today—still wild and home to the same species of wildlife.

"I think of how tough and rugged he must have been, wearing just a skin cloak, carrying tools he probably made himself," Bill says.

Bill is pretty tough and rugged himself, an avid and passionate wilderness hunter. A Sparwood, British Columbia schoolteacher, he hunts elk in the East Kootenay region, in the same country where, in the early 1900s, one of his (and our Continent's) conservation heroes, William T. Hornaday, used to hunt. With a love for the wild gained through hunting, Bill helped found the Hornaday Wilderness Society and is working to protect and conserve the same wildlands that he, and Hornaday, and many others have hunted, or currently hunt, or will (we hope) hunt in the future.

As Bill told me about *Kwaday Dan Sinchi*, imagining that long ago hunter's plunge into oblivion, he said: "If I should fall and die in the wilds, God forbid, I would only hope that if my remains are found long into the future, they would be found by fellow hunters still pursuing wild animals in country still wild."

If there are to be hunters and wild places to hunt in the future, we must understand and cultivate our heritage. *What we understand, we can honor and sustain.* Read this book, and pass it on.

DAVID STALLING,
Hunting writer, president of
Montana Wildlife Foundation,
Trout Unlimited field staff

INTRODUCTION

> *"We have not too many monuments of the past; let us keep every bit of association with that which is highest and best of the past as a reminder to us, equally of what we owe to those who have gone before and how we should show our appreciation."*
>
> THEODORE ROOSEVELT
> NOVEMBER 16, 1903 [1]

I took to the hunt because somewhere within my nature there throbbed the rhythm of the chase. To satisfy the urge I wandered wild places, *rifle in hand*, for more than fifty years. I took to wild places with the exuberance of a pup, eager to embrace the physical and spiritual nourishment offered by sprawling prairie, brushy draw, rolling foothills, and deep mountain mass. Through five decades I killed and savored the gift of wild things. The thought of paying it back never occurred to me, because, at the time, I had no idea where it came from.

Through most of a lifetime I harbored a casual belief that being a hunter was simply part of forever. I never paused to ask how, why, or who. In time the hunt became a search for those answers. After a half-century afield it became important to know how the animals reached my time, why our culture valued them, and who made them important. The hunt became more than a seasonal pursuit of recreation and sustenance; it became a search for truths buried in our nature and embedded in our culture.

The hunt now called for a new fulfillment—tracking and finding the truth of history. How was it I could be a hunter? Why were field and forest laden with game? Who were the people that passed such a rich legacy to me and my fellow hunters in North America? What I learned, first amazed and then excited me. The full dimension of what it meant to be an American hunter began to explode in my mind. The saga of the American hunter began to emerge as the greatest environmental achievement of any human culture—ever. The euphoria of that conclusion, however, refused to excuse me from the required reality check. Is everything okay out there on the wild landscape? Will there always be a hunt? Will the 21st Century bring a new truth to our times? The short answer to all these questions is yes. However, serious challenges face those of us who dream of passing a heritage of ethical, sustainable, fair-chase hunting into a space-age world.

To appreciate how hunting came to us, a quick trip through time and history is helpful. Native cultures hunted the North American continent for perhaps 150 centuries. In the last two-and-one-half of those centuries, a new nation, the United States of America, proclaimed its existence. When America was new, our forefathers were a handful of colonists who declared their independence from the most powerful nation on earth. They were a people with a burning belief in a concept articulated by English philosopher John Locke. The idea was simple enough: *perhaps all men were created free and equal before God and each other.*

In 1776 freedom and equality were radical thoughts. It took a Declaration of Independence, a Revolutionary War, a United States Constitution, and a Bill of Rights to validate these ideas and launch the American aspiration. These founding actions and documents did not address fish, wildlife, hunting, or fishing. Our opportunity to be hunters and anglers, however, soon emerged as part of being an American. The opportunity to hunt and fish was destined to be part of *life, liberty, and the pursuit of happiness*, words that Thomas Jefferson penned into the preamble of our Declaration of Independence.

Rifle in Hand is a sample of a few rich stories now woven into the fabric of our American hunting legacy. They are tales plucked from a stream of events involving hunters as the American hunting heritage took root and then found its way from Bunker Hill to our time.

The idea that fish and wildlife would belong to all the people of the United States emerged from a series of court decisions. The debate over who might own fish and wildlife reached the U.S. Supreme Court a mere 66 years after the Declaration of Independence. In that early case, the court settled a dispute about gathering oysters in the New Jersey Meadowlands. The high court favored a common oysterman over a property owner. An important precedent was thus seeded: in the new land, fish and wildlife were not to attach to property, but to the people. Throughout American judicial history, fish and wildlife have been ruled the people's resource, to be held and managed by the states as a public trust for the common good.

Probably the single most important American to take to the hunt was Theodore Roosevelt, the 26th President of the United States. He was the greatest conservationist any society has ever known, and he savored life while spending it, in his words, "*rifle in hand.*" His thoughts and deeds anchor this story. Comparing Thomas Jefferson and Theodore Roosevelt, historian Stephen Ambrose noted: *"Jefferson loved music and playing the violin, while TR's principal hobby was rifles and hunting."* Roosevelt's influence, overpowering in his time, continues to be felt in the American spirit to this day. He was a hunter, and from the hunt came his vision for building a nation that would, as he put it, *"last through the ages."*

When the 20th Century began, Roosevelt became our youngest president ever. When he entered the White House in 1901, the idea of conservation had not yet found its way into the public mind. When he left office in 1909, he had implanted the idea of conservation into our culture and enriched our future prospects with 230 million acres of designated public forests, wildlife refuges, bird preserves, parks, national monuments, and game ranges. While Roosevelt was leading the way in the United States, Prime Minister Sir Wilfred Laurier advanced similar policies and ideas in Canada. In unison they were creating a uniquely North American endeavor that influenced wildlife conservation throughout the world.

These gifts of protected wild places and the animals that came to live there have found their way to our time. As a young hunter, I had no idea my hunt was connected to all these people, events, and places. When I began to realize they were, I 'did the math' and learned that TR was born sixteen years after the Supreme Court decided fish and wildlife in America would belong to the people. Sixteen years after TR's death, I was born. I was now beginning to appreciate that wildlife in America, and my opportunity to give chase, were no longer simply part of forever. Hunting, fishing, and our public lands are part of a fragile experiment *unlike anything else tried in human history.* All of it, conducted through what is little more than a twinkle in time, an experiment—like our democracy itself.

In the pages that follow there are stories about a few other important American hunter-conservationists. All of them, the great, the less famous, and the quiet legions that escape mentioned here dedicated themselves to two basic principles. The first is that hunting in America would be for everyone because wildlife belonged to everyone. The second is that wild animals could be brought back from the edge of the oblivion where market killers and commerce left them when the 19th Century ended.

This writing also includes some personal reflections, stories that helped me understand the value of hunting in America. What we understand, we can honor and sustain. Only by fully understanding our past will we be prepared to meet our obligation to take the hunter's heritage forward to another generation. What follows is what I learned about how hunting came to our time and to me. With minor adjustments, it is the story of every North American who goes afield, *rifle in hand.*

THE TRAIN FROM LITHUANIA

A nature writer once likened humanity to water striders on the surface of a pond. He described us as creatures suspended between two eternities, the pond our past and the sky our future. After living a half-century thinking primarily of the present and what might be next, it came time to explore the depths of my own pond. For me, those murky depths had been of no particular interest. Now I wanted to know how my family came to America. I also looked to find what other truths lived in the unvisited depth. Specifically, I looked to learn how the joy of the hunt, and the landscape that nurtured the hunter and the hunted, came to fill my life.

Elkhorn Peak, Montana, can usually be seen on the horizon as I pass along a narrow lane through the forest that connects my home to a county road. The Elkhorn Mountains became part of America's forest reserves in 1905. More than sixty years later I hunted and then shot a bull moose in those mountains. Events connecting my family history to that moose hunt began in Eastern Europe about the time Theodore Roosevelt took the oath of office as our nation's Vice-President. It was March of 1901.

Horribly sick, my grandfather Antonus Pacevicus (Anton Posewitz), made his way to a cool, clear spring deep in the forest outside of Vilnius, Lithuania. The young peasant knew the spring and the renewing strength he could draw from its chill waters. Twenty-seven years of age, the forest was almost all he knew, but he knew it well. The forest, his wife Anna, and *'the train'* were the dimensions of his life. Antonus fell heavily into the moss beside the spring, desperately gulping its water to heal his nausea, clear his clouded brain, and calm his pounding heart. For two days and nights he lay there, moving only to take of the spring and vent the sickness he had forced upon himself.

It was *'the train.'* The train had come to Vilnius with the Czar's soldiers to conscript peasants for the Russian army. The Trans-Siberian Railroad was under construction and it manifested the Czar's desire for territory and a warm-water port. It also created a demand for troops during the Boxer Rebellion. The Czar's politics saw an advantage if the casualties would be Lithuanian rather than Russia's own sons. In 1901 the railroad was nearing Port Arthur and many would die there in the Rebellion and the Russo-Japanese War that followed. Somehow Anton knew that if *'the train'* took him, he would never see Anna again. The term of conscription in the Czar's army was 25 years.

The image of *'the train'* forever haunted Antonus' memory of the *'old country'* and he carried that dark memory to his grave. My imagination sees a dimly lit railroad platform, a clanking black engine coughing smoke and spewing steam into the chill blackness of a spring night, the Czar's soldiers herding confused peasants into wooden cars reaching down the tracks.

Chewing tobacco and swallowing the juice had induced Antonus' sickness. The sickness was real enough and the ruse worked. He was not taken, and later the cool spring water cured him. Before *'the train'* could return, the young man left his pregnant wife behind and made passage to America. The Russo-Japanese War's climactic battle of Shenyang occurred

Rifle in Hand

in February and March of 1905; 330,000 Russian soldiers engaged their adversary and 90,000 of the Czar's conscripts died. By May 17th the Russian fleet entered the combat only to be annihilated in the battle of Tsushima Straight; 4,000 sailors went down with their ships.[1] Antonus had made a good choice.

For a fare of $50 my grandfather took a different ship, the *Victoria*, and landed in Baltimore on the Fourth of July 1901. 'Antonus' became Anton. Like many eastern European immigrants, Anton found work in a Pennsylvania coal mine. In March of 1901 the political ticket of President William McKinley and Vice President Theodore Roosevelt had entered the White House. On September 16th of that same year the Pennsylvania Railroad provided the funeral train that brought the assassinated President McKinley's body from Buffalo, New York, to Washington, D.C. The new American President, Theodore Roosevelt, was aboard, and the route carried them through the troubled coalfields of eastern Pennsylvania. Biographer Edmund Morris described the scene and circumstance in his book *Theodore Rex*:

> Then one cut gave way to the shaft of a coal mine, and for a few seconds Roosevelt...could exchange stares with four hundred filthy coal miners....Boys, youths and old men...stood bareheaded, leaning on picks and shovels. Their small, smudged eyes...squat bodies, and tape-wrapped shins proclaimed them to be Slavs....Implicit in the stare of those eyes, the power of those knobby hands, was labor's historic threat of violence against capital.[2]

Rifle in Hand

I now wonder if one of those '*filthy coal miners*' was my grandfather. Morris also wrote that if 1901 was a good year, a miner could expect to earn $500, less company deductions. After a year in the mine, Anton saved enough to bring Anna and her newborn, my 'Uncle Tony,' to America. When the violent coal strike of 1902 shut down the mines, Roosevelt introduced America to a new relationship between labor and management, the '*Square Deal.*' Including the miner's interest in the government's intervention in labor negotiations must have given my grandparents confidence, for in 1903 my Aunt Teresa became the first in my family to be born in America. In 1906 Anton moved the family to Sheboygan, Wisconsin, and took up work in a chair factory. He exchanged coal dust for sawdust and lived to be ninety. That same year my father John Anton was born. Forty-seven years after my father's birth, I boarded a train for Montana. Eighteen-year-old James Anton, John and Marie's youngest son and one of Anton and Anna's grandchildren, went west.

I came west in 1953 with a passion to be a hunter, and I found land and wildlife to satisfy the longing. Seventeen years later, after eleven days of searching, tracking, and stalking through Montana's snow-locked Elkhorn Mountains, I killed a bull moose. Returning the next day with a sled and six great-grandsons of Anton and Anna, we brought in a full year's supply of meat from the forest. The oldest son, Eric Anton, pulled the meat-laden sled from the lead position.

Montana was among the places Theodore Roosevelt hunted. In an article published in 1893 he wrote:

> hunters, who…penetrated…this wilderness, found themselves in…hunting grounds…much the same as their lusty barbarian ancestors followed, with

weapons of bronze and of iron, in the dim years before history dawned. As late as the end of the seventeenth century, the turbulent *village nobles of Lithuania and Livonia* hunted the bear, the bison, the elk, the wolf and the stag, and hung the spoils in their smoky wooden palaces: and so, two hundred years later, the *free hunters of Montana*...hunted game almost or quite the same in kind, through the cold mountain forests.... (emphasis added) [3]

On May 12, 1905, President Theodore Roosevelt signed an executive order placing the Elkhorn Mountains into America's National Forest Reserve. Those mountains thus became part of the public estate where the descendants of European peasants could enjoy and savor an activity that was once reserved for those of noble birth. TR was clear when he laid down the philosophy that would guide the restoration of wildlife in America. His words, published that same year, were:

> Above all, we should realize that the effort toward this end is essentially a democratic movement. It is...in our power...to preserve large tracts of wilderness...and to preserve game...for...all lovers of nature, and to give reasonable opportunities for the exercise of the skill of the hunter, whether he is or is not a man of means. [4]

Anton was not a *'village noble'* nor were we ever people of *'means.'* My grandfather was a resourceful peasant smart enough to stay off *'the train'* and bold enough to bring his family to a land where all people, by virtue of their own daring declaration of equality and independence, were *free and equal before God and each other.* Finally, hunting through the cold mountain forest, I was beginning to understand and appreciate what it meant to be an American and to be among Roosevelt's *free hunters of Montana.*

Last of the Buffalo Hunters

My desire to be a hunter in the mid-20th Century was tempered by concern about whether or not the game would be there once I found my way to field and forest. Although I didn't know it at the time, I could have been more patient. Wildlife across America was well on the road to recovery during my youth and each year things were getting better. It was an altogether different story during Theodore Roosevelt's time.

In the year of TR's birth, 1858, there were 10 Americans per square mile in our young nation. According to some estimates, there were also about 17 buffalo per square mile. In 1900, when TR was a candidate for vice-president, there were 25 Americans per square mile and the buffalo had been slaughtered to near extinction. A remnant herd of 20 to 40 wild bison held on in marginal sanctuary in Yellowstone National Park.[1]

When President-elect William McKinley and his new Vice President Theodore Roosevelt rode to their inauguration on March 4, 1901, they declined to ride in one of the nation's 10,000 automobiles. They declined because automobiles were not reliable enough to get them up Pennsylvania Avenue.[2] The transport, technology, and commercial incentives of the time, however, had been adequate enough to strip the continent of 60 million buffalo and most of our other big game.

When TR reached the presidency as a result of McKinley's assassination in September of 1901, he was our youngest president ever. During the 42-year period from TR's birth to his presidency, commerce in wild animals and their body parts produced a slaughter unprecedented in human history. The tragedy reached across the breadth of our nation from the Atlantic to the Pacific. Deer in the eastern United States were so scarce at the dawn of the 20th Century that the following account by John M. Phillips, a Pittsburgh hunter and in time a conservationist, was reported in Joe Kosack's *History of the Pennsylvania Game Commission:*

> About six inches of snow had fallen, so we tracked it all day, camped on the trail that night, followed it all the next day then rested over night at the town of Brockwayville. In the morning, we took up the trail again and succeeded in jumping and killing the buck. During all that long chase, we didn't cross another deer track. I said to my friend, 'I am done—I think I have killed the last deer in Pennsylvania.' [3]

Fortunately, resistance to the commercial exploitation of wildlife was growing among the fledgling sport hunting community. Addressing trends in recreation and the wildlife profession, authors John Organ and Eric Fritzell reported:

> By the late nineteenth century, sportsmen's organizations and publications (e.g., *Forest and Stream*) had coalesced into a social movement led by elites that pressed for an end to commercial traffic in wildlife and for government oversight of wildlife conservation.[4]

Rifle in Hand

The commercial and subsistence carnage of America's wildlife happened to coincide with TR's life and his development as a person, a hunter, and a public servant. Roosevelt's life included an early interest in natural history that never diminished. Out of his interest in nature evolved a passion for the hunt. In his book, *Theodore Roosevelt the Naturalist*, Paul Russell Cutright notes:

> No one turned the boy's face...to the open forest. He struck out by himself, took his own bearings, and was never so far diverted by other interests as to lose his course.[5]

When TR entered Harvard in 1876 and the nation celebrated its first centennial, buffalo hide shipments down the Missouri River from Fort Benton, Montana, peaked at 80,000 hides.[6] It was the same year that Lieutenant Colonel George Armstrong Custer met his demise on the banks of Montana's Little Big Horn River. The times and the face of our nation were changing. At that point, young Roosevelt had been to Europe and floated the Nile of Egypt, but he had not yet seen the American West.

Although Roosevelt had not been west, the urge to do so had been firmly planted in his mind from the time he learned to read. As a boy, while struggling with asthma and a generally frail physical condition, he read voraciously. Biographer Nathan Miller describes the early signs of TR's western attraction:

> Away to the wild West! These words set Teedie's vivid imagination afire. In his dreams he escaped to the prairies and mountain ranges beyond the rolling Mississippi.[7]

Upon graduation from Harvard, Roosevelt ventured beyond the Mississippi to taste the American West for the first time, and he went there to hunt. Using Chicago as a base, TR and his brother Elliott hunted as far north and west as Minnesota's Red River. It was the edge of the northern Great Plains, a place where the western landscape takes form only to fade beyond an always visible, yet distant, horizon. The brothers hunted birds and almost surely wondered what lay beyond the shimmering horizon teasing them ever westward. Biographer Miller reports the following account:

> '(We) are travelling on our muscle and don't give a hang for any man,' Theodore reported. But the hunting was not as good as he had hoped, and his asthma returned. Both his guns broke, and he was bitten by a snake and thrown out of a wagon on his head.' [8]

It was TR's first taste of the west, and like most young hunters there were skills to be developed. For now, the North Dakota Badlands, the Missouri River Breaks, and the shining mountains of Montana, Wyoming, and Idaho awaited another time. I cannot help but believe that when the Roosevelt brothers turned their wagon back toward Chicago, TR turned to face the setting sun.

Had TR and his brother gone a little further west to the Missouri River they would have witnessed the downstream flow of buffalo hides. The big muddy river drained an enormous geographic expanse, and in the 1880s its boats and barges were draining the spoils of a wildlife slaughter. It was occurring on a landscape that had sustained aboriginal hunters since the late Pleistocene.

Rifle in Hand

There was more than water going down river. Somewhere out beyond North Dakota's far horizon the market hunters were into the last of their continental pillage. Hides from the northern buffalo herds were streaming down the Missouri. The shipments from Fort Benton, Montana, that peaked at 80,000 hides when TR entered Harvard in 1876 collapsed to zero by 1884. The great American Plains fell deathly still. The grunts and roars of the bison that played across the Great Plains for 15,000 years were gone. The stripped carcasses rotted in the searing sun, and only the wind broke the silence. However, a few scattered buffalo remained in remote places, and Roosevelt was in hot pursuit.

In 1883, TR made plans to hunt wild buffalo before the opportunity was lost forever. It was a chance to be one of the last buffalo hunters. Although his wife Alice was expecting a child and a companion canceled out at the last minute, Theodore would not be deterred. The prospect of being a hunter of buffalo was fading fast and TR likely did not even consider missing his chance. Alone, TR boarded the train west. While realizing a boyhood dream, young Roosevelt was unknowingly launching a new American hunting heritage. Writing at the time that he was *"anxious to kill some large game—though I have not much hope of being able to do so"*[9] suggests he may have seen his chance to be among the last hunters fading or perhaps already gone. The prospect of recreational hunting for the people of our relatively young nation was perilously close to ending forever.

In September of 1883, TR stepped off the train into the North Dakota Badlands near the Little Missouri River. The great herds of buffalo were gone, but the passion to hunt them was not. After eight days of futile searching he cut the track of a lone buffalo. The intensity of the pursuit can only

Theodore Roosevelt, 25 years old.   HERITAGE PHOTOGRAPHIC, TUCSON, AZ

be imagined. Roosevelt couldn't wait to share the news with his expectant wife Alice and he couldn't contain his exuberance. He wrote to her: *"Hurrah! The luck has turned at last. I will bring you home the head of a great buffalo bull, and the antlers of two superb stags."* He concluded the letter with: *"I am in superb health, having plenty of game to eat, and living all day long in the open air. With a thousand kisses for you, my own heart's darling I am ever your loving, Thee."* [10]

The next year, 1884, followed a fateful course and ended with TR back in North Dakota. In the time between, he had won re-election to the New York Assembly, celebrated the birth of a daughter, and survived the devastating emotional collapse that came with the death of his wife and the death of his mother. Two of the most important people in his life had died in the same house on the same day. Dabbling in national politics that autumn also turned into disappointment. At the end of it all, TR wrote a compatriot: *"I don't believe that I shall ever be likely to come back into political life."* Placing his young daughter Alice Lee in the custody of his sister, TR returned to the American frontier to restore his body and spirit.

Back in North Dakota where he had invested in a cattle herd and a land partnership, TR's energy was directed to the business of ranching and his passion for hunting. He wrote a friend:

> I heartily enjoy this life, with its perfect freedom, for I am very fond of hunting and there are few sensations I prefer to that of galloping over these rolling, limitless prairies, *rifle in hand*, or winding my way among the barren, fantastic and grimly picturesque deserts of the so-called Bad Lands. [11]
> (emphasis added)

Rifle in Hand

Roosevelt's experiences over the next few years supplied material for three of his 35 books: *Hunting Trips of a Ranchman, Ranch Life and the Hunting Trail,* and *The Wilderness Hunter.* The hunt, including taking considerable quantities of game for subsistence, was the daily routine. TR hunted of necessity, for the pure joy of it, and for the exhilaration that came from *the strenuous life.* In the process, the eager mind of a naturalist saw the expanse of the American continent, and he saw it through the eyes of a hunter.

What Roosevelt saw was the need to rescue wildlife from the death spiral of commercial killing that brought an entire continent's big game resource to the brink of extinction. Biographer Nathan Miller observed that TR's conservation vision for wildlife restoration had been *"…an idea that had begun with a lonely hunt in the Bad Lands."* More likely, the idea had been nurtured through his association with George Bird Grinnell, owner and editor of the weekly sporting journal *Forest and Stream.* Outdoor sporting periodicals that emerged in the 1870s were championing the concept of a sporting code for North American hunters.[12] Had Theodore Roosevelt not been captured by the idea of a *sporting code* to couple with his conservation vision, his generation might well have been remembered as America's last hunters.

The Conservation Idea

While Roosevelt's vision for wildlife conservation matured on his hunts through the American West, it was a vision shared by few of his countrymen. A French nobleman, Alexis de Tocqueville, visited America in the 1830s to study the new democracy that was only sixty-some years old. To many Europeans, the new form of governing in America was viewed as interesting but still experimental. Upon his return to France, de Tocqueville published *Democracy in America*, in which he observed:

> In Europe people talk a great deal of the wilds of America, but the Americans themselves never think about them; they are insensible to the wonders of inanimate nature. Their eyes are fired with another sight; they march across these wilds, clearing swamps, turning the courses of rivers....[1]

Perhaps de Tocqueville perceived a flaw in the democratic notions fueling the engines of a young nation recently born of revolution. Early in the 19th Century there was little indication that America would find a conservation ethic solid enough to place land and resources in trust for all the people. The idea of setting aside public lands that would in time nurture national forests, a wilderness system, parks, national monuments, wildlife refuges, bird sanctuaries, game ranges, and hunting for every American was almost beyond anyone's imagination. Our exuberant ancestors might well have made a physical mess of nation building had it not been for a handful of thoughtful, politically astute, and conservation-minded Americans.

There were two critical ideas embedded in our nation's history that made conservation possible. When those ideas were coupled with Theodore Roosevelt's energy, philosophy, penchant for reform, and the bully pulpit of his presidency, our national conservation character was formed.

The U.S. Supreme Court germinated the first critical idea, the concept that fish and wildlife in America were to be held as a public trust. The first U.S. Supreme Court decision defining that trust was issued in 1842, sixteen years before TR's birth. The court drew its guidance from custom since the time of Magna Carta, common law, and the American Declaration of Independence. In addition to settling disputes, the law—refined and reinforced through litigation—justified the action that was to come.

The other critical idea was advanced in the writings of George Perkins Marsh, George Bird Grinnell, and a handful of others who were mostly sport hunters. In his book *Man and Nature*, Marsh linked the fate of failed civilizations to their inability or unwillingness to temper their impact on nature. Marsh's book has been called the "fountainhead of conservation." Theodore Roosevelt was five years old at the time of its publication in 1863.

With the publication of the periodical *Forest and Stream* in 1873, Grinnell and others had a platform for advancing the idea of a hunting code based on sportsmanship. Grinnell, who had hunted the West a decade before TR's adventures there, became a close associate of Roosevelt. In comparing experiences, they realized the changes that had occurred in wildlife populations in that time. In 1887 Grinnell and TR invited nine fellow hunters to a dinner that resulted in the formation of the Boone and Crockett Club. The year before, Grinnell had published an editorial that led to the creation of the Audubon Society.[2]

Getting the American people to adopt a conservation ethic, however, was the monumental step. That step had to wait until TR was our president. When his opportunity came, TR responded by using the need to protect forests, watersheds, and wildlife for every American as both the practical and motivational themes for introducing America to conservation.

First: Wildlife as a Public Trust

When the American colonists liberated us from the control of the king of England, they were focused on liberty, individual freedoms, and creating a system in which free people could govern themselves. The issues of water, fish, and wildlife were not mentioned in our Declaration of Independence, Constitution, or Bill of Rights. The legal void was filled by a series of court decisions.

The critical first argument involved a New Jersey oysterman engaged in a dispute with a landowner about access to water and oysters in the *'New World.'* The landowner, Mr. Waddell, sought to prevent an oysterman, Merritt Martin, from gathering oysters in New Jersey's tidal marshes. Waddell traced his property title back to a land grant made by the king of England to his brother James, the Duke of York. The land grant occurred when the colonies were still part of the British Empire. In the language of those times, the grant included the *"fishings, hawkings, huntings and fowlings."* The question was whether or not these royal perks survived the American Revolution as privileges of private property ownership. In Martin v. Waddell, the Court was faced with deciding whether or not the American custom of gathering from the commons would be sustained. The highest court of our emerging nation ruled:

> When the revolution took place, the people of each state became themselves sovereign; and in that character, held the absolute right to all their navigable waters, and the soil under them; for their own common use, subject only to the rights since surrendered by the constitution to the general government.
>
> When the people of New Jersey took possession of the reins of government, and took into their own hands the powers of sovereignty, the prerogative and regalities which before belonged either to the crown or the parliament, became immediately and rightfully vested in the state. [3]

In a later case involving illegal game animals being taken across state lines, the U.S. Supreme Court got wonderfully more specific. The case was Geer v. Connecticut (1896) and the court's ruling included the following language:

> ...the development of free institutions has led to the recognition of the fact that the power or control lodged in the State, resulting from the common ownership, is to be exercised, like all other powers of government, as a trust for the benefit of all people, and not as a prerogative for the advantage of the government, as distinct from the people, or for the

benefit of private individuals as distinguished from the public. [4]

These court cases laid down legal precedent for the idea that fish and wildlife cannot be owned as private property but are to be held in trust by the government for the benefit of all people. It was the legal framework in which George Perkins Marsh and George Bird Grinnell applied their intellectual talent, and where, later, Theodore Roosevelt exercised his political leadership. To help us follow the historical time line, the Connecticut case was decided nine years after TR founded the Boone & Crockett Club and two years before he led the charge up San Juan Hill.

Second: Man, Nature, and the Sportsman's Code

In 1800, on Mount Tom near Woodstock, Vermont, forest slash left behind by cut-out and move-on logging burned. A year later, George Perkins Marsh was born. Son of an attorney and 'gentleman farmer,' the scholarly young Marsh grew up watching the mountain trying to emerge from its own ashes while being grazed by sheep and cattle. He also watched flash floods erode the slopes and carry away the family bridge and sawmill. One flood swept away a new woolen mill he had built.

The Marsh family was politically active, and George held seats in the Vermont Legislature and the U.S. Congress. President Zachary Taylor (1849-1850) later appointed Marsh ambassador to Turkey. While serving as ambassador, Marsh was able to indulge his intellectual interests in ancient civilizations, weather, and nature. Biographer David Lowenthal wrote of Marsh's time in the Middle East:

Rifle in Hand

Marsh sensed man's antiquity in every quarter....It was here Marsh first realized that man had everywhere left his mark; in time he saw how far that touch had transformed nature. [5]

In ancient civilizations Marsh began to see Vermont and all of America in fast-forward. It was a vision of what human civilizations had done to landscapes, to nature, and ultimately to themselves. What he saw was the emergence of civilizations, the exploitation of nature to sustain them, followed by their collapse. It was a predictable sequence: emergence, prosperity, desert and doom. In Marsh's mind, Mount Tom, eroding hillsides, and flash floods were all part of this pattern.

Marsh soon realized that man had everywhere left depleted landscapes in his wake, and he saw how significantly the human presence had transformed nature. Marsh synthesized his wide experiences into *Man and Nature,* a plea and a blueprint for the conservation of nature in America—at the time still a *'New World.'*

George Bird Grinnell was born in Brooklyn, New York, in 1849. When he was ten years old his father bought property on the estate of naturalist-artist John James Audubon. On that property young George enjoyed his first hunts. During his life Grinnell would hunt extensively in the American West. One of his hunts included the pursuit of buffalo with the Pawnee Indians; it turned out to be their last buffalo hunt. In 1874 he rode with George Armstrong Custer into the Black Hills of South Dakota. Fortunately for conservation in America, Grinnell declined an invitation to accompany Custer in 1876.

The year of Custer's fateful expedition, Grinnell took the job of natural history editor for *Forest and Stream.* In

1880 he purchased the weekly sporting newspaper and became its editor-in-chief. At the time the publication was the most popular journal of its kind. Through this journal Grinnell became an untiring advocate for hunting seasons, bag limits, license fees, conservation principles, and the sporting code. Writing in a 2002 article, Leonard H. Wurman states:

> While names such as Theodore Roosevelt, Gifford Pinchot and John Muir are bandied about as originators of the conservation movement, it was really George Bird Grinnell who influenced, directed and solidified it more than anyone. [6]

Today we read the writings of conservation pioneers Gifford Pinchot and Theodore Roosevelt for insight and guidance. Who did Pinchot and Roosevelt read? They read Marsh and they read Grinnell—weekly. Pinchot called *Man and Nature "epoch-making."*[7] Few individuals had more influence on the forest conservation thinking of Theodore Roosevelt than Pinchot did. He was "America's Forester" and the U.S. Forest Service's first chief.

Bringing it all Together

As the 20th Century neared, a number of Americans were convinced that the nation needed a conservation ethic. Among them were Roosevelt, Pinchot, Grinnell, William T. Hornady, and other prominent citizens. All these people held a common desire to protect wildlife and wild places; they were also all hunters. The problem they faced was winning the hearts and minds of the people. As TR observed early in his presidency:

Rifle in Hand

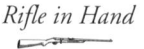

> The idea that our natural resources were inexhaustible still (persisted), and there was as yet no real knowledge of their extent and condition. The relation of the conservation of natural resources to the problems of National welfare and National efficiency had not yet dawned on the public mind.[8]

Roosevelt's observation was nearly identical to that made by the French nobleman de Tocqueville 28 years before TR was born. In his autobiography Roosevelt would later observe:

> The Conservation movement was a direct out growth of the forest movement. It was nothing more than the application to our other natural resources of the principles, which had been worked out in connection with the forests. Without the basis of public sentiment which had been built up for the protection of the forests, and without the example of public foresight in the protection of this, one of the great natural resources, the Conservation movement would have been impossible.[9]

These assessments of the 'public mind' or consensus early in the 20th Century paint a picture of the prevailing temperament when TR served as president. The courts had ruled that fish and wildlife were not *'property'* but belonged to all the people and were to be managed as a public trust. The nation had a small cadre of conservation thinkers, nearly all of them hunters. The wisdom of Marsh's idea to respect nature easily led to the need to protect forests and watersheds. Land protection, along with the utilitarian logic of the forest's potential for renewal, held considerable public appeal. Finally,

Rifle in Hand

America had a hunter in the White House dedicated to the tasks of public education and direct action to launch our nation's conservation agenda. In his autobiography, Gifford Pinchot qualified Roosevelt for the task of conservation leadership by writing, *"He was an outdoor man—more a wilderness hunter."* [10] It was a time of nation building and our nation began to embrace the principles of conservation when addressing the use of America's natural resources.

Taking Action

"I admire men who take the next step, not those who theorize about the two-hundredth step."

Theodore Roosevelt

As the conservation idea developed in the minds of recreational hunters, we were not yet a nation committed to the restoration of game animals. In order to sell conservation to the nation, our leaders leaned on the practical logic of renewable forests and functional watersheds as practical educational tools. However, hunting was the passion driving the people who committed themselves to the task. Game was becoming scarce, and through the 1880s poachers continued to penetrate some of the early sanctuaries set aside for wildlife, including Yellowstone National Park. The monetary value of buffalo hides and heads escalated as extinction of the species became a distinct possibility. Throughout this decade, Roosevelt continued to expand his own hunting horizon, now penetrating the deep mountains of Montana, Idaho, Wyoming, and British Columbia.

As Roosevelt's skills and experiences as a hunter expanded, so did his determination that the hunt would not vanish with his generation. A good example of his growing dedication occurred in 1886. TR contacted a former market hunter living in western Montana about a mountain goat hunt. He wrote: *"I want to shoot a white antelope goat. I have heard it is the hardest animal in the Rockies to find and the most difficult to kill."* The purpose of the letter was to engage John Willis as a guide. However, John was having trouble reading TR's handwriting and responded, *"If you can't shoot any better than you can write, No."* Undeterred, TR came anyhow. The trip was arduous, Roosevelt shot several goats, and the two hunters became life-long friends. It was reported of the trip that:

> Theodore talked constantly to Willis, who made his living slaughtering game for their hides, about the necessity for conserving wildlife....Theodore...made of him a staunch believer in conservation and he ceased to be a game butcher but became a strong worker for its preservation.[1]

Later, as President, TR had occasion to visit Butte, Montana. Willis was in the crowd that greeted Roosevelt at the railroad station. To get Roosevelt's attention and make a point of their friendship, Willis called out, *"My God, Theodore, where did you get that pot belly?"* Continuing, Willis added, *"You know I made a man of you and now you are spoiling my work."* Roosevelt, reveling in seeing his old hunting guide, seized the opportunity to remind Willis of his conversion to conservation by responding, *"Yes, and I made a Christian of you and don't spoil my work."*[2]

One year after the goat hunt, Roosevelt was back in New York with like-minded associates forming the Boone and Crockett Club for the preservation of big game in North America. Two years after that, in 1889, TR accepted an appointment as the U. S. Civil Service Commissioner from President Benjamin Harrison. Before moving to Washington,

Rifle in Hand

Roosevelt went west one more time, perhaps to be the last buffalo hunter.

The hunt began at the head of Montana's Wisdom River. It is reported that he "*hunted them faithfully*" but without success. It is probably just as well since 1889 was the year Montana closed the season to the killing of bison. However, TR did encounter a small group of buffalo just south of the Montana border in Idaho, and he killed one. Remembering the stalk, Roosevelt wrote:

> I watched the great, clumsy, shaggy beasts….Mixed with the eager excitement of the hunter was a certain half melancholy feeling as I gazed on these bison, themselves part of the last remnant of a doomed and nearly vanished race. Few, indeed, are the men who now have, or ever more shall have, the chance of seeing the mightiest of American beasts, in all his wild vigor, surrounded by the tremendous desolation of his far-off mountain home. [3]

Wildlife and those who hunted them had clearly reached the critical fork in the trail. Their choice was to take and record the last of the big game species, or launch an effort to preserve and restore them.

Within a year of killing that last, or nearly last, wild buffalo, Roosevelt and his colleagues in the Boone and Crockett Club began meeting with important congressmen to protect the wildlife of Yellowstone National Park. All were aware that a small number of buffalo were still alive in the park, but so were poachers. The handsome fees paid by taxidermists who believed the species would soon be extinct provided all the motivation a poacher required. In September of 1894, an *"Act to Protect the Birds and Animals in Yellowstone National Park,"* introduced by Congressman John Lacey of Iowa, completed its journey through Congress and into law.[4] The wild bison of Yellowstone, among the last remnants of what TR described as *"a doomed and nearly vanished race,"* won a reprieve. Congressman Lacey, like TR, was an outdoorsman and member of the Boone and Crockett Club. The recreational hunter's hand had just been extended to pull wild bison back from the abyss of extinction. The club was also instrumental in creating the New York Zoo so future generations could see big game animals of the American West in case they were driven to extinction in the wild.[5]

TR's commitment to the salvation of buffalo continued into his years as president. In June of 1905 he designated the Wichita Game Preserve in Oklahoma. Shortly after doing so he received word from a Comanche Chief noting the absence of buffalo. The Chief wrote, *"Tell the President that the buffalo is my old friend, and it would make my heart glad to see a herd once more roaming about."*[6] Roosevelt had 15 prime buffalo selected from the New York Zoo and sent to the Oklahoma preserve, where their progeny now number about 600.

Wildlife conservation was a matter of taking direct action in the late 19th and early 20th centuries. The immediate strategy was to create refuges and extend protection with whatever tools could be mustered to do the job. The idea of wildlife conservation through the protection of entire landscapes was also within the vision of early activists. Again, forestry with its utilitarian attraction of protecting watersheds for clean water and generating renewable timber crops was the popular vehicle. The legal means for addressing extensive landscape conservation came with an 1891 revision of the nation's land laws. The revision allowed the president to set aside woodlands as part of a national system of forest reserves. George Bird Grinnell and Gifford Pinchot of the Boone and Crockett Club, along with their leader Theodore Roosevelt, vigorously promoted the legislation. This legislation was known by the short title: "*The Forest Reservation Creative Act of 1891.*" [7] Ten years later, when TR became our president, the *'Creative Act'* suddenly rested in the hands of one of its creators. Roosevelt used the act's authority to increase our national forest reserves from about 43 million acres to more than 190 million acres. No president, before or since, has done more.

The President's frenetic pace of direct action did not preempt his educational mission. Roosevelt was determined to use education to embed a conservation ethic befitting the nation's potential as a 'new world' democracy. There was little doubt about who the beneficiaries of the conserved landscape were to be. TR's nation-building pride, with all the grandeur it engendered, was always anchored to the people. The common Americans were to be the beneficiaries of the American commons. Roosevelt's vision, now a blend of conservation ideas and personal experiences, was remarkably consistent with court rulings on public trust responsibilities. This vision for America, carried in TR's words, span a century with the crystal clarity of a mountain morning:

> The movement for the conservation of wildlife, and the larger movement for the conservation of all our natural resources, are essentially democratic in spirit, purpose and method. [8]

> It is foolish to regard proper game-laws as undemocratic, unrepublican. On the contrary, they are essentially in the interests of the people as a whole, because it is only through their enactment and enforcement that the people as a whole can preserve the game and prevent its becoming purely the property of the rich who are able to create and maintain extensive private preserves. The wealthy man can get hunting anyhow, but the man of small means is dependent solely upon wise and well-executed game-laws for his enjoyment of the sturdy pleasure of the chase. [9]

> We do not intend that our natural resources shall be exploited by the few against the interests of the many....Our aim is to preserve our natural resources for the public as a whole, for the average man and the average woman who make up the body of the American people.[10]

When TR spoke of the inclusive nature of the democratic approach to conservation he was also considering posterity—that turns out to be you and me and those who follow us.

> The 'greatest good of the greatest number' applies to the number within the womb of time, compared to which those alive form but an insignificant fraction. Our duty to the whole, including the unborn generations, bids us restrain an unprincipled present-day minority from wasting the heritage of these unborn generations. [11]

1903 Theodore Roosevelt in Yellowstone.
THEODORE ROOSEVELT COLLECTION, HARVARD COLLEGE LIBRARY.

Rifle in Hand

Theodore Roosevelt's first term as our president was the unfinished term of assassinated President William McKinley. When TR ran for election in 1904 the *New York Sun* editorialized: *"Roosevelt steps from the stage gracefully. He has ruled his party to a large extent against its will."* The Sun editorial then went on to single out TR's conservation record. *"And, then, there is the great and statesmanlike movement for the conservation of our National resources, into which Roosevelt so energetically threw himself at a time when the Nation as a whole knew not that we are ruining and bankrupting ourselves as fast as we can.... This globe is the capital stock of the race.... Our forests have been destroyed; they must be restored.... These questions are not of this day only or of this generation. They belong all to the future."* The editorial concluded with a rhetorical question: *"What statesman in all history had done anything calling for so wide a view and for a purpose more lofty?"* [12] When the vote was tallied, Theodore Roosevelt was elected our President by the largest margin in American history.

The people loved that president, and that president stood for the people. To do so, he often stood alone against the will of politicians in his own party as well as his partisan opponents. The gifts he left his people were a public land estate of 230 million acres, 9.9 percent of America. It was a public estate the size of Texas—plus Kentucky and Connecticut—and a wildlife resource that belongs to all Americans. It was, and it still is, the people's game.

The conservation momentum thus created became continental in scale. Canada's Prime minister, Sir Wilfred Laurier, was in accord with Roosevelt's principles. In 1911 Sir Clifford Sifton, one of the country's most powerful civil servants, headed a Canadian Commission on Conservation.

Rifle in Hand

It is worthy of note that Canada, a colony known for its loyalty to the 'Mother Country,' adopted the American model of wildlife conservation and not the one of England, where the ownership of game went from royalty to property owner.[13]

We are now a century past planting the conservation ethic in the American culture. Is the ethic still embedded in the people? It sure is! In April of 2003 a local newspaper carried a story under the headline, *"Marines feast on gazelles from Saddam's preserve."* The military was camped near the deposed dictator's private hunting grounds near Tikrit, Iraq. The troops embellished their field rations by hunting and eating royal gazelles. The cook was Corporal Joshua Wicksell of Corpus Christi, Texas, a man skilled in the preparation of game. The heart of this story was the observation that: *"Each…platoon has been limited to killing one gazelle a day to make sure the herd isn't depleted."*[14] This restriction may be the first time in the history of human warfare that a conquering army came with both an overwhelming military capacity—and a wildlife conservation ethic. In this case, the U.S. Marine Corps and Corporal Wicksell carried the hunter/conservationist ethic.

The Great Occasions

"It was a very lovely morning, the sky of cloudless blue, while the level simmering rays from the just-risen sun brought into fine relief the splendid palms which here and there towered over the lower growth."
                                        Theodore Roosevelt

Thus dawned the day, July 1, 1898, that Theodore Roosevelt called *"the great day of my life."* TR was on the verge of what he considered to be his *"crowded hour."*[1] It was a term he used to identify a point in a person's life where all the character, skill and substance of a person are tested to such a degree that it defines the individual. For TR, the standard usually applied to combat where life and death were in the equation. The 'great day' of 1898 cost the lives of many young American and Spanish soldiers. The prize was San Juan Hill, the high-ground over looking Santiago, Cuba. Theodore Roosevelt's Rough Riders were among the combatants.

The idea of a "crowded hour" was one way to test a person's response to a threat or challenge. It was TR's belief that in order for a man to emerge as a leader, that person would have to engage a challenge worthy of his attributes. As he stated it: *"If there is not the great occasion, you don't get the great statesman."*[2] In the context of wildlife restoration, Roosevelt's *'great conservation occasion'* involved using the power of the presidency to set aside an enormous public estate, press the idea of conservation into the American mind, and then pass his conservation vision to the people. In his autobiography TR describes an event he created to involve the states and, through them, conservation minded people of grassroots America:

> ...I wrote to each of the Governors of the several States and to the Presidents of various important National Societies concerned with natural resources, inviting them to attend the conference, which took place May 13 to 15, 1908, in the East Room of the White House. It is doubtful whether, except in time of war, any new idea of like importance has ever been presented to a Nation and accepted by it with such effectiveness and rapidity, as was the case with this Conservation movement when it was introduced to the American people by the Conference of Governors. The first result was the unanimous declaration of the Governors of all the States and Territories upon the subject of Conservation, a document which ought to be hung in every schoolhouse throughout the land. [3]

It took a generation or two before a 'Conservation Pledge' eventually did find its way into American schoolhouses. However, the conservation idea, and responsibilities inherent in that idea, were sent from the White House to the people. Many states already had fish and game conservation agencies while others, moved by the President's urging, responded to the call.

Immediate actions resulted in more and better resources for wildlife law enforcement along with the creation of state, county, and local refuges. In order to be effective, however, enforcement had to be coupled with changing attitudes, traditions and habits. Individual restraint was now required for the common good. This did not happen naturally in a young nation still bent on conquering the wilderness. It was time for a new generation of leaders to step forward and address the *'great occasion'* of their time. A few stories of some remarkable people who pioneered fish and wildlife conservation need to be told. Our opportunity to be hunters might not have made it to our time had they not responded to the wildlife conservation challenges of their time. One individual confronted his 'great occasion' in the cause of wildlife conservation in South Carolina. His is a remarkable tale.

Rifle in Hand

Alfred Aldrich Richardson
"The Chief"

South Carolina entered the 1900s facing the prospect of restoring wildlife, modifying public attitudes, and protecting the habitat that once produced fish and wildlife in abundance. In an article titled "The Prodigal Years," published in *South Carolina Wildlife* magazine, the condition and attitude of those times is described: [4]

> Gone were the wolf and cougar, the epitome of true wilderness. The elk, the bison and the beaver had also departed. The majestic ivory-billed woodpecker soon would exist in memory only, a fate already shared by the passenger pigeon and the brilliantly plumed Carolina parakeet. The wood duck, the Eastern wild turkey and the white-tailed deer were

refugees seeking sanctuary in the deepest riverbottom swamps.

...most citizens were either indifferent or actively opposed to restrictions on the taking of game. Game laws were few and those that did exist meant little, if for no other reason than the apparatus to enforce them was nonexistent.

Theodore Roosevelt was recognized as *"a tireless proponent for preservation."* The magazine went on to note that the formal establishment of South Carolina's wildlife department in the wake of TR's presidency was *"more than chronological coincidence."*

In 1910, less than two years after Roosevelt's Governor's Conference, the South Carolina legislature passed Act No. 293 providing *"the execution of the bird, game and non-migratory fish laws of South Carolina shall be by and under the direction of a commissioner, to be known as the Chief Game Warden."* It was the birth of South Carolina's wildlife department following the period described as *"prodigal years."*

On March 7, 1913, the second person to head the agency walked through the door; he was Alfred Aldrich Richardson. Mr. Richardson proved to be special. He was destined to hold the position of Chief until 1958 and, in the process, set a high conservation standard. A.A. Richardson's 45-year career was a classic example of a man of principle and character responding to a long list of *great occasions*. Those occasions included a few *crowded hours*.

In 1905, the year TR began his second term, South Carolina made provision for having a game warden in each of the state's 46 counties. When Richardson took office in

Rifle in Hand

1913, he traveled the state to assess the impact the wardens were having. He believed that wardens needed to teach the conservation ethic as well as enforce the law. His findings on both counts were disappointing. Finding little respect for the law, he concluded that some *"weeding"* was necessary. *"He immediately and dramatically reduced the force of wardens, many of whom were honorary appointees who did nothing. One of the first removed from office was Richardson's own father."* It was obvious from the beginning that a new day was dawning in wildlife conservation.

Early in the Chief's career he was offered a $1,500 bribe *"to make certain that the Belmont Plantation in effect remained a fiefdom with guarantees of no unwelcome intervention from wardens."* An angry Chief responded, *"I'll stoop to no bribes."* Later the Chief's first annual report noted: *"Among those arrested for not having a nonresident license, with the case being made by the chief game warden personally, were August and Morgan Belmont and their close friend, F. M. Carnegie—all industrial magnates and some of America's wealthiest, most powerful men."* A valuable lesson was probably learned in this episode since August Belmont later earned a reputation as a committed conservationist and is reported to have had a genuine respect for Mr. Richardson. As for the "Chief," not only would he not be bribed, he also made it clear that conservation was for everyone and there would be no people of special privilege. It would be just as Roosevelt so often described—this was going to be a democratic endeavor. Conservation and hunting, the effort and the reward, were to be shared.

Early in Richardson's career, while attending a baseball game, a group of six hard-core poachers physically attacked the Chief. The newspaper reported that while he was *"efficiently making pacifists of his assailants,"* one got behind him and stabbed him in the back. A friend came to Richardson's aid, holding the attackers at bay with a handgun and getting the bleeding combatant to a hospital. It took the Chief months to recover from his wound. It also happened to be a good example of how the 2nd Amendment to the U.S. Constitution was working early in the 20th Century.

Before Richardson took over the South Carolina Wildlife and Marine Resources Department in 1913, its annual revenues amounted to less that $2,000. By 1915 revenues had grown to nearly $45,000, agency morale was soaring, and a new order of professional conservation was emerging. Along the way Richardson employed his considerable political skill to get things done. One incredible story occurred in 1949 when he arranged to restock the Piedmont area with white-tailed deer. After much publicity, 1,000 people arrived to witness the release. They barbecued *"seventeen hogs, three goats and a number of beef cattle."* On hand to participate in the release of deer and mingle with the largest crowd the rural site had ever seen was the Governor of South Carolina, Strom Thurmond. It was the same Strom Thurmond who went on to be our country's longest serving U.S. Senator, serving eight terms and retiring in 2003, one month after his 100th birthday.

A.A. Richardson guided his department through two world wars, an economic depression, the introduction of the first resident hunting and fishing licenses, creation of a state fish and game commission, department expansions in response to the Pittman-Robertson and Dingell-Johnson Acts, and many other significant conservation issues. During his career he was subject to three legislative investigations and the overt hostility of one governor. The Chief survived all challenges.

In the 1920s the legislature formally established that all wildlife was the property of the state and that harvesting game was a privilege to be managed and administered by the state on behalf of the public. It was a proclamation that easily suited Richardson who believed the state had, in his own words, *"a moral obligation to the people to conserve their valuable natural resources."* Near the end of his career Richardson exceeded the state's mandatory retirement age and an annual legislative exception had to be secured to enable him to continue. Every year it was granted.

While "The Chief" was indeed an exceptional person rising to the *great occasions* of his time, South Carolina's conservation legacy included many individuals with deep commitments to fish and wildlife. Richardson's leadership and integrity created an environment in which each of them could function to their fullest. History attests that those individual abilities were and still are substantial.

Jay Norwood Darling
"D'ing"

From Theodore Roosevelt's presidency through the 'Roaring Twenties,' hope was hatching in the depleted wood lots, forests, marshes, and meadows of America. Then, with little warning, the entire nation seemed to collapse. Drought-parched western states gave birth to a new phenomenon, the 'Dust Bowl.' Black clouds of fine dirt from the Great Plains blew eastward across an entire continent. As if in sympathy for the pain of the sod-busted prairie, our financial institutions collapsed into their own black cloud, the 'Great Depression.' It was a major setback for wildlife as grasslands and wetlands withered and hungry people took to subsistence hunting just to survive. The times are remembered as the 'Dirty Thirties,'

Rifle in Hand

and the nation needed a conservation revival. This need became another man's *great occasion;* he was Jay Norwood (D'ing) Darling.

Jay Norwood Darling was born on October 21, 1876 in Norwood, Michigan, a remote village on Grand Traverse Bay of Lake Michigan. The year of Darling's birth was a significant milepost in American wildlife history. In addition to being our nation's first centennial, 1876 was the year Native Americans killed Custer in the Battle of the Little Bighorn, Theodore Roosevelt began his college education at Harvard, and the buffalo hide shipments down the Missouri River from Fort Benton, Montana, peaked at 80,000 hides.

After several moves the Darling family settled in Sioux City, Iowa, when Jay was 10 years old. It was there, where the fertile Iowa uplands rolled out to the banks of the Missouri River, that Jay Norwood Darling developed a conservation ethic along with a unique talent as an illustrator. In the 1880s, Iowa was at the edge of America's fading wilderness, and nowhere would change be more dramatic than in the tall grass prairies of our heartland. Darling biographer David Lendt reported: *"As a boy, Jay saw the stern-wheelers loaded with bales of raw buffalo hides for the Saint Louis Market."* [5]

Darling's youthful experiences in the grasslands also involved watching civilization's impact on golden plovers, prairie chickens, and waterfowl in Iowa and South Dakota. These experiences moved Darling to conclude: *"It was the disappearance of all that wonderful endowment of wildlife which stirred the first instincts I can remember of conservation."* [6] Roosevelt was ranching in western North Dakota and hunting there and into the Northern Rocky Mountains at the same time young Jay romped through head-high grass in Iowa and South Dakota. Jay's gift was the ability to draw, and the young

Iowan nurtured that talent in spite of the fact that his parents were not enthusiastic. He once related to a friend: *"To my father and mother artists who drew pictures were classed with wicked playing cards, dancing and rum...."* [7]

During his formative years Jay spent his summers working on an uncle's Michigan farm. It was a place he remembered as a *"youthful paradise,"* having a clear fishing stream running through it along with productive wood lots and marshes. Years later, returning to attend his uncle's funeral, he found the farm depleted and barren. He wrote: *"This was my first conscious realization of what could happen to land, what could happen to clear running streams, what could happen to bird life and human life when the common laws of Mother Nature were disregarded."* [8] What George Perkins Marsh had observed on Vermont's Mount Tom and in collapsed civilizations of the Mediterranean, Darling saw just as clearly on Uncle John's Michigan farm. Biographer Lendt observed: *"Theodore Roosevelt and Gifford Pinchot later fired his determination with their courageous endorsement of conservation principles and their condemnation of those who violated the tenets of good stewardship."* [9]

In his quest for a higher education Darling gave as well as he took. His first year was spent at Yankton College, South Dakota, where he was kicked out for 'borrowing' the college president's horse and buggy. The next stop was Beloit College, Wisconsin, where as managing editor of the school paper, his transition to journalism began. He also worked on the Beloit yearbook where he substituted his character sketches for the traditional photographs of the faculty. This outrageous act led to a year's suspension. Biographer Lendt observed: *"They did not appreciate the sketch of a revered professor of Latin singing, 'There'll Be a Hot Time in the Old Town Tonight'."* [10] Darling

Rifle in Hand

This cartoon shows Ding's basic conservation belief—that man can benefit from nature without damaging it.
J.N. "DING" DARLING FOUNDATION

signed his creation D'ing, a contraction of his last name that stuck for life. The song just happened to be the 'official' song of TR's Rough Riders. Returning to Beloit to make a speech in the 1950s, D'ing set the record straight: *"The truth is I was not fired because of that picture, but because I flunked damn near every study I took that year."*

After a delayed graduation Darling became a reporter for the *Sioux City Journal* where his writing and illustrating skills took root. While at the *Journal* he published the first of his many editorial cartoons. Among his first was one that included a man he very much admired—Theodore Roosevelt. In 1906 Darling moved up to the *Des Moines Register and Leader* where his career flourished as a reporter, editorial cartoonist, and conservationist. Through the first half of the 20th Century his drawings appeared in nearly 150 newspapers and his creative images had an enormous impact. It was a period that saw two world wars, a drought, the Great Depression, application of Theodore Roosevelt's 'Square Deal' for workers, Franklin D. Roosevelt's 'New Deal' for depressed America, and finally the reawakening of a national conservation ethic. None of these *great occasions* escaped Darling's participation—or D'ing's potent illustrations.

It was during the 'Dirty Thirties' that Darling began to address a full menu of *great occasions*. During that dirty decade, he worked to take the Iowa Fish and Game Commission out of politics and then he served on the Commission. The change of state law that he found so necessary was providing the state wildlife agency protection from direct political control. In the 1930s the Iowa Fish and Game Commission law became a model for the nation. As a commissioner he pioneered creation of the Cooperative Wildlife Research Unit at Iowa State University and launched the preparation of a

25-year conservation plan for Iowa. Under Darling's leadership the planning effort was placed in the hands of another native Iowan—the great conservationist Aldo Leopold.

In 1934 Darling accepted President Franklin D. Roosevelt's appointment to head the U.S. Biological Survey, forerunner of the U. S. Fish and Wildlife Service. In 1935, in collaboration with a group of industrialists with an interest in hunting, he succeeded in getting financing for the Cooperative Wildlife Research Units, the American Wildlife Institute, the first North American Wildlife Conference, and the National Wildlife Federation.

In creating the Federation, Darling stated that hunters and anglers *"should have some kind of harness to band them together to exert a united influence for the good of wildlife."* Darling left government service to be the first president of the National Wildlife Federation. Within a year the Pittman-Robertson Wildlife Restoration Act passed the U.S. Congress and provided the financial fuel for the recovery of wildlife. The Act, supported by the hunting industry and the rank and file hunters, placed an excise tax on firearms and ammunition, and the resulting revenue was made available to states. However, to qualify for the federal aid, the Act also required that the states retain all of their hunting license income in their wildlife programs. The Wildlife Restoration Act went from its introduction in Congress to President Franklin Roosevelt's signature in only ninety days. It was the culmination of a host of goals laid out in the 1930 American Game Policy that called for de-politicized state wildlife agencies, creation of a wildlife profession, and stable funding. The federal legislation was skillfully drafted by Carl Shoemaker of Oregon and carried by A. Willis Robertson of

Virginia and Key Pittman of Nevada. During our nation's darkest hours for wildlife, help was generating across the continent.

Darling and a host of associates were responding to a lot of *great occasions* and we now enjoy the fruit of their having passed before us. Near the end of his life D'ing observed, *"I'm learning one thing the hard way, and that is that you have to re-educate the public mind about every fifteen or twenty years or it forgets everything learned a while back."*[11] There is a lot truth in that statement and North American hunters were blessed with an educator/philosopher who responded to a unique challenge—our education and our intellectual development.

D'ing died February 12, 1962 and left us one last gift, an illustration wishing us adieu. J.N. "DING" DARLING FOUNDATION

Rifle in Hand

Aldo Leopold
"The Father of Game Management and the Land Ethic"

The year TR shot one of America's last free-ranging bison in Idaho, Jay Norwood 'D'ing' Darling was a twelve-year-old in western Iowa growing up on the banks of the Missouri River near Sioux City. On the bluffs above the Mississippi River near the eastern Iowa city of Burlington, Aldo Leopold was a two-year-old just sampling the simple wonders of life. Theodore Roosevelt, South Carolina's A. A. Richardson, and D'ing Darling were all politically active and more than just a little combative. Each rose to the *great occasions* of their times with exuberant vigor. What Aldo Leopold brought to the movement was science, vision, thoughtful reflection, and beautiful writing. Leopold, an avid hunter, was able to advance a philosophy that established a valid relationship between human hunters and nature. In the context of extending hunting into the 21st Century, Leopold's intellectual legacy has become as valuable as the physical restoration of wildlife that characterized the 20th Century.

Aldo Leopold, university-trained as a forester, joined the U.S. Forest Service in 1909. It was the same year Roosevelt left the presidency and went on an African safari. When Roosevelt set sail for Africa, he left the 190-million acre national forest resource in the hands of Gifford Pinchot, chief of the U.S. Forest Service. It was an idealistic moment for the new agency and our nation's first professional foresters. As one of them, Aldo Leopold rode off to the American West determined to introduce and employ a land conservation ethic as a matter of national policy.

When Leopold stepped off the train at Springerville, Arizona, as a representative of the public interest in public resources, he found depleted wildlife, overgrazed ranges, locally exhausted timber, and active erosion. All this had happened in only 23 years, since the Army had captured Geronimo and brought an end to the Apache defense of Arizona's high plateau and canyon country. That defense had kept white settlers at bay. Biographical writer Peter Wild summed up Leopold's reaction as well as his relationship with his new associates: *"the young Leopold recognized the problem, while others busied themselves with making it worse."*

Leopold spent the next fifteen years in the Southwest where his attention was inescapably drawn to wildlife and wildlands conservation. In 1924, he convinced the Forest Service to set aside one-half-million acres as wilderness in the Gila National Forest.[12] This administrative action was taken forty years before Congress passed the Wilderness Act. Aldo

Leopold was thinking ahead of his time and it would be a long while before an American majority would have the foresight and humility to see the necessity to protect wildlands for posterity. When Leopold managed to take that farsighted action it was one of conservation's *great occasions*. Years later, writing about the root of the wilderness idea, he left us the following record. *"The earliest action I can find in my files is a letter dated September 21, 1922, notifying the District Forester that two local Game Protective Associations had endorsed the establishment of a wilderness area on the head of the Gila River, in the Gila National Forest."* [13]

When Theodore Roosevelt went west to hunt, wilderness was simply a condition of the unsettled American frontier. Thirteen years after TR left the White House, the idea of retaining wilderness in America was moving from theory to reality, and Aldo Leopold found the call for action in local Arizona rod and gun clubs. Clearly, the damage to grasslands and forests that Leopold had seen was also of concern to recreational hunters. One historian noted, *"Leopold looked at wilderness through the eyes of a hunter and budding ecologist."* [14] When he did, he saw and then he argued, *"Wilderness areas in the National Forests would serve especially the wilderness-hunter...."* [15]

Years later Aldo Leopold gave considerable thought to the essence and substance of wildlife management in America. At the time he wrote:

> Good professional research in wilderness ecology is destined to become more and more a matter of perception; good wilderness sports are destined to converge on the same point. A sportsman is one

who has the propensity for perception in his bones. Trigger-itch, wanderlust, and buck-fever are simply the genetical raw materials out of which perception is built. [16]

Theodore Roosevelt's passage from young naturalist to hunter and then on to America's consummate conservationist certainly fits Leopold's dictum.

A man of Leopold's vision became uncomfortable in the bureaucracy of the Forest Service. In 1928 Aldo left, and the agency lost its best thinker. Leopold, then living in Madison, Wisconsin, went to work conducting game surveys for the Sporting Arms and Ammunition Manufacturers Association. At the time there was no such thing as a science-based wildlife profession. Five years later, responding to the challenge of another *great occasion*, Leopold wrote the book, *Game Management*, and it was wildlife management's first text. A profession was being born and Aldo Leopold will forever be known as its father.

Two years later, not willing to trust the government with the wilderness idea, Leopold helped create The Wilderness Society. The idea of preserving wild lands on a national scale was thus invested, not in the government, but in the people. The Wilderness Act did not become law until fifteen years after Leopold's death. The people, however, were true to the idea and prevailed. Wilderness could now be one of the people's *great occasions*. America entered the 21st Century with 104.7 million acres (4.4 percent of our nation's land) in the protective custody of congressionally designated wilderness.

Leopold settled in at the University of Wisconsin to teach the first generation of professional wildlife managers.

Rifle in Hand

He also bought an exhausted piece of farmland on the banks of the Wisconsin River. A reclaimed chicken coop became the family's 'shack,' and they restored the depleted land back to ecological health. In the process of reflecting on his experiences as a forester, biologist, and custodian of a riverbank farm, Leopold wrote *A Sand County Almanac*. The book is a collection of essays on our relationship with the land, the biotic community, and the future. For those of us who continue to draw inspiration from the writings of this thoughtful hunter, the *Almanac* was perhaps Leopold's greatest contribution.

Leopold died of a heart attack on April 21, 1948, while fighting a grass fire near his shack shortly after receiving word that Oxford University Press would publish the *Almanac*. He never saw his most notable work in print. When I entered college in 1953 to begin my studies in fish and wildlife management, Leopold's *Game Management* was the text. I was gifted my first copy of *A Sand County Almanac* that same year. The science of game management has changed considerably since 1933; however, the philosophy articulated in *A Sand County Almanac* appears timeless.

In the Epilogue of *American Sportsmen and the Origins of Conservation,* historian John Reiger writes:

> Leopold, Roosevelt, and Grinnell grew up in a sportsman's world, where they not only had abundant opportunities to hunt and fish, but where they learned to accept responsibility for the game and its habitat.

Rifle in Hand

Reiger concludes with the observation:

> In perceiving how the land ethic evolved out of the code of the sportsman and the continuing tradition of the sportsman-conservationist ideal, we acquire not only a deeper understanding of Aldo Leopold, but on the whole history of American conservation.[17]

The quiet, thoughtful Aldo Leopold responded to the challenge of our conservation education and honing our conservation perceptions as a *great occasion*. He wrote:

> All ethics so far evolved rest upon a single premise: that the individual is a member of a community of interdependent parts....The land ethic simply enlarges the boundaries of the community to include soils, waters, plants and animals, or collectively: the land.

Perhaps no one will ever say it better than that.

Taft, Peril and Posterity

Since conservation of a nation's resources seems such a straightforward, proper thing to do, it is a wonder that it remains such an ongoing struggle. Public opinion consistently comes down on the side of conservation, clean air, pure water, and prudent resource management. At the same time, we remain locked in cultural combat trying to realize Leopold's ethic where *"the boundaries of…community…include soils, waters, plants and animals, or collectively: the land."*

The dark side of *"the land"* equation is the view of land not as community but as commodity. It is the view of land as simply real estate, no more than a place to gather timber, minerals, oil, natural gas, and forage. In addition, once wildlife was restored to America's landscape, commercial interests in wildlife quickly returned with a renewed persistence. While trade in buffalo hides and tongues had collapsed, the commercial interest in wildlife did not. While conservationists were restoring the people's game animals, commercial interests were redesigning their business models about how to exploit them.

Before addressing the present and our future prospects as hunters, one more historic tale needs to be told. It is the story of Theodore Roosevelt and his good friend and presidential successor, William Howard ("Big Bill") Taft. The story of TR and Taft needs telling because it holds the political lesson we must never forget. To tell this tale we must return to the late 1890s and the early 1900s.

Rifle in Hand

Very few politicians embraced the progressive principles of conservation when the 20th Century was new. Roosevelt's reforms changed everything, but it didn't take long for special interest groups to design a new strategy for getting at the public resources. The tactic was simple: gain political influence and use it to affect public policy. Even before TR left the White House, the natural resource entrepreneurs set their sights on "Big Bill."

To help us appreciate the story of Taft, it is necessary to first consider the unique political nature of Theodore Roosevelt. It is a great story and an important part of our hunter's legacy.

Roosevelt's Political Character

Theodore Roosevelt was a maverick in his time and, sadly, a political anomaly since. One biographer described TR's choice of political party as follows: *"The prejudices of birth and inheritance directed him to the party that had in his childhood saved the union…the Democrats offered little. Bad as the Republican organization was, Tammany, by reputation was worse."* [1] Just as Roosevelt had little enthusiasm for either major political party, they had even less for him.

Events leading up to Roosevelt's nomination to be Vice President of the United States in 1900 provide an excellent example of political party machinery at work and its discomfort with Roosevelt. In 1898 during the Spanish American War, TR and his Rough Rider regiment charged up and took San Juan Hill. The event was dramatic and Roosevelt's war-hero status led to him being elected Governor of New York. By the time Roosevelt finished his first year as governor, the New York Republican Party bosses were already distressed by his commitment to reform. One state party leader, in urging TR's nomination for Vice President of the United States, put it this way: "*I want to get rid of the bastard. I don't want him raising hell in my state any longer. I want to bury him."* [2] On the other hand, industrialist Mark Hanna, Republican national party boss and U.S. Senator from Ohio, expressed the party's misgivings by stating: *"Don't you realize that there's only one life between that madman and the White House?"* [3]

With the election of the McKinley-Roosevelt ticket in 1900, the strategy of *'burying'* Roosevelt seemed to be working. As vice-president, TR realized his worst nightmare—boredom and isolation. His own words at that time were: "*The vice president....is really a fifth wheel to the coach....It is not a stepping stone to anything but oblivion."* [4] It might have been the end of the line for the progressive ideals of perhaps the only politician with enough energy, patriotism, character, and will power to move a nation—alone if he had to. It might have been the end of the line, except for the dastardly deed of an anarchist—Leon Czolgosz.

On September 6, 1901, Czolgosz shot President William McKinley. Eight days later McKinley died of the wounds. The Rough Rider's Colonel, who had been *'buried'* as Vice President, got a chance to lead the nation. Mark Hanna's worst nightmare was being realized. His comment was, *"Now look, that damned cowboy is President of the United States."*

Hanna's statement was true enough. One other thing was also true: *a hunter was President of the United States.* The stage was set for a whole new spectrum of *great occasions* for the 'Colonel,' now our nation's president. Among the opportunities would be conservation of the nation's resource capital and restoration of its wildlife. As president from 1901 to 1909, TR impacted the American landscape and its future with the following actions: 1) Supported and then signed the National Monuments Act; 2) Designated eighteen national monuments including Niagara Falls and the Grand Canyon; 3) Created with Congress five new national parks; 4) Designated big game ranges in Oklahoma, Montana, Arizona and Washington; 5) Set aside fifty-one bird sanctuaries; 6) Increased the forest reserves from 43 million to more than 190 million acres; and, 7) Established the U.S. Forest Service and named Gifford Pinchot its leader.

When it was all added up, it was a wildlands estate of 230 million acres under public protection. No President, before or since, ever did more for conservation. TR was doing it so every American could *"enjoy the sturdy pleasure of the chase…whether we were or were not men of means."* A hunter and patriot was in the White House who believed all people '*were created free and equal before God and each other,*' just like the American Declaration of Independence proclaimed.

TR made one huge mistake when he was elected President in 1904. After learning the results of his smashing victory he said: *"The wise custom which limits the President to two terms regards the substance and not the form, and under no circumstance will I be a candidate for or accept another nomination."*[5] When the 1908 election approached, he wished with all his heart that he had not made that statement.

Unlike some contemporary politicians, Roosevelt lived by his word, and members of Congress knew he would. They knew Roosevelt's power was passing, and powerful industrial interests were already at work to diminish his reforms. In his autobiography Roosevelt observed: *"When my successor (Taft) was chosen, however, the leaders of the House and Senate, or most of them, felt that it was safe to come to a break with me, and the last or short session of Congress, held between the election of my successor and his inauguration four months later, saw a series of contests between the majorities in the two houses of Congress and the President—myself—quite as bitter as if they and I had belonged to opposite political parties. However, I held my own."*

Because of the public support Roosevelt enjoyed, the choice of a successor was his and he chose "Big Bill" Taft. TR and Taft were more than political associates. Taft, a large hulk of a man, had served President Roosevelt in a number of capacities and the President genuinely liked and trusted him. Biographer Edmond Morris described the President's wife's concern about their friendship. *"Edith Roosevelt worried about the growing fondness of each man for the other. When Theodore asked Taft for advice, what he usually got was approval."* Because of this fondness for one another, and the President's aggressive nature, Taft was easy to dominate—and easy to hurt.

Described as a Roosevelt 'Yes Man,' Taft, on the campaign trail for his own presidency, put it this way, *"I agree heartily and earnestly with the policies which have come to be known as the Roosevelt policies."* [6] When the time came, TR worked hard on Taft's behalf. He did his work so well that when the Republican Party convention came to order in 1908, Taft had a lock on 563 delegates, 72 more than was needed to nominate. There was only one more scare left for those anxious to see TR leave. When Henry Cabot Lodge mentioned Roosevelt's name during the convention's keynote address, a spontaneous chant from the delegates of *"Four, four, four years more"* threw the convention into pandemonium. Roosevelt, however, had told the people in 1904 that he would not seek another term in 1908. While the convention delegates, the electorate, and TR himself wished another term, a man of honor had given his word.

Rifle in Hand

Taft walked off with the nomination and won the election. Taft's alienation with TR began almost immediately. The estrangement soon separated the two presidents and it holds a lesson for us as we address the present. Just as a century ago Taft was asked to carry the legacy of Roosevelt, we as heirs to the American hunting heritage now inherit the task of carrying that legacy forward into the new century. Our challenge is to do better than 'Big Bill.'

While some of Roosevelt's Cabinet wished to remain in their positions, Taft appointed new people more likely to be loyal to his presidency. Roosevelt Biographer Nathan Miller described this transition as follows: *"Though puzzled and hurt, the president accepted this decision.... 'Ha ha! You are making up your Cabinet,' Roosevelt chortled on the last day of the year. 'I, in a lighthearted way have spent the morning testing the rifles for my African trip. Life has its compensations.'"* However, as he was cleaning out his office, TR confided to a prominent journalist his opinion of his friend Taft. *"He's all right. He means well and he'll do his best. But he's weak. They'll get around him."* [7] TR had become a flawless judge of character.

Life's compensations for TR always seemed to revolve around the hunt. Taft's inauguration was in March; by late April Roosevelt was on a train carrying him from Mombasa across Africa's Kapiti plain. The route of the Uganda Railway passed through a game-rich landscape. To have an unobstructed view of the land and its wild beasts, TR had a seat attached to the engine's cowcatcher and that is where he rode. The 'Colonel' was free and riding an iron horse across Africa—he went *'rifle in hand.'*

Back in Washington Taft continued to replace key Roosevelt appointees. In the Interior Department, a Seattle-area promoter was appointed to replace the strong conservationist then heading the agency. Shortly after the change, an Interior Department investigator unearthed a plan under which the new Secretary intended to turn over Alaska coal lands to an industrial syndicate. The investigator took the information to Gifford Pinchot and Pinchot sent him directly to the new President. Taft's response was to fire the investigator. Pinchot responded by taking the information public through a series of news leaks.

A short time later, a native runner moved with rhythmic grace across the African savanna. The runner carried breaking news and his destination was Roosevelt's camp. TR was hunting white rhino, and the news was important enough to dispatch a runner. The news had traveled from Washington, D.C., to a remote hunting camp in the African Congo in ten days. What news was so important? Taft had fired Gifford Pinchot!

Roosevelt's friend and most trusted conservation collaborator was out. *"I cannot believe it,"* Roosevelt wrote Pinchot, *"I do not know any man in public life who has rendered quite the same service you rendered...."* In his autobiography TR reflected: *"Gifford Pinchot is the man to whom the nation owes most for what has been accomplished as regards the preservation of the natural resources of our country."*

Taft also shut down the forestry education program originally described by TR as an effort *"to make all the people of the United States acquainted with the needs and the purposes of practical forestry."* The trust Roosevelt had placed in Taft had been violated, and an estrangement between the two men became personal, political, and nearly complete.

Before returning to the United States, Roosevelt toured Europe, and Pinchot met him there to bring him up to date on events. It was in Paris that Roosevelt gave the speech containing one of his most memorable passages.

> The credit belongs to the man who is actually in the arena, who strives valiantly, who knows the great enthusiasms, the great devotion, and spends himself in worth causes. Who at best, knows the triumph of high achievement and who, at worst, if he fails, fails while daring greatly so that his place shall never be with those cold and timid souls who know neither victory nor defeat.

The 'Rough Rider' was preparing to re-enter the fray and perhaps he suspected the political odds were long—and now against him.

In 1912, Roosevelt challenged Taft for the Republican nomination for President. Although TR still held strong support among the party voters, the party 'machine' controlled most of the delegates and denied Roosevelt the nomination. In the general election of 1912, Roosevelt formed a third political party and ran for president as the Progressive (Bull Moose) Party candidate. TR beat Taft soundly, but the Democrats beat the divided Republicans and Woodrow Wilson became America's 28th President.

The great affection that TR and Taft once shared was genuine, and time allowed their bitter estrangement to heal. Six years after the 1912 campaign, a chance meeting of the two occurred in a hotel dining room. Biographer Miller describes the scene:

> Roosevelt was intent on his meal, but sensing a sudden hush, looked up and saw Taft's smiling face looming over his table. Immediately throwing down

his napkin, he rose, hand extended. They shook hands vigorously and eagerly slapped each other on the back. The other guests applauded, and suddenly realizing they had an audience, the two ex-presidents bowed and smiled.

The next year on January 6, 1919, Theodore Roosevelt died in his sleep. His son Archie cabled his brothers that *"The Old Lion is Dead."*

On a cold, gray January day, Roosevelt was laid to rest on a frozen site in the Young's Memorial Cemetery overlooking Oyster Bay, on New York's Long Island. Patchy snow covered the ground as pallbearers carried the flag-draped, plain oak casket slowly up a gentle slope. An American giant was being laid to rest. Politicians, Rough Riders, and hunting companions trudged shoulder-to-shoulder up the hillside. In the gathering dusk after all others left the burial site, one lone figure remained. It was a hulk of a man dressed in the black of mourners, his head tilted forward, his sagging shoulders heaving as he wept. It was 'Big Bill' Taft. The man Theodore Roosevelt selected to carry his legacy forward, the person trusted as a friend, and the person just not able to live up to the expectations of a giant was left alone—weeping over a hero's grave.

We are left to wonder what demons passed through Taft's mind. We can only speculate as to the echoes he heard at that moment, which of his decisions or concessions of principle returned to haunt his memory. Ultimately, we must wonder which of those tortured recollections did 'Big Bill' carry to his own grave.

Finally, how about us? What is the lesson of Taft for us? We are also heirs to a significant portion of the Theodore

Rifle in Hand

1919 burial of Theodore Roosevelt, Youngs Memorial Cemetery, Oyster Bay, NY. THEODORE ROOSEVELT COLLECTION, HARVARD COLLEGE LIBRARY

Roosevelt legacy. We, those of us privileged to take to the field *'rifle in hand,'* are entrusted by fate and circumstance to hold and nurture the hunter's legacy. We must put our minds to thinking about where and how we will stand on TR's principles of conservation, on his principles of hunting, and on his clearly articulated principles of American democracy—including hunting for everyone.

THEODORE ROOSEVELT'S PRINCIPLES OF THE HUNT

…preserve large tracts of wilderness…and game…for all lovers of nature, and…for the exercise of the skill of the hunter, whether he is or is not a man of means.

…the conservation of wildlife, and…all our natural resources, are essentially democratic in spirit, purpose and method.

Public rights come first and private interests second.

…the genuine sportsman…is by all odds the most important factor in keeping…wild creatures from total extermination.

The true hunter…loves all parts of the wilderness….

A peculiar charm in the chase…comes from the wild beauty of the country….

…the rich…who are content to buy what they have not the skill to get by their own exertions—these are…the real enemies of game.

When hunting him (wapiti)…He must be followed on foot, and the man who follows him must be sound in limb and wind.

…skill and patience, and the capacity to endure fatigue and exposure, must be shown by the successful hunter.

I wish to preach, not the doctrine of ignoble ease, but the doctrine of the strenuous life….

This cartoon was drawn at the death of D'ing Darling's friend Theodore Roosevelt in 1919. D'ing idolized Roosevelt for his early work in conservation and establishment of the country's first National Refuge during his presidency. J.N. "DING" DARLING FOUNDATION

The Hunt That Must Survive

As America closed out the 20th century, we looked across a landscape rich with wildlife. Recreational hunters had assumed responsibility for the welfare of game animals and both prospered through a century. If there was an omission, it was that we lost sight of the people and the principles that carried us through the challenges and obstacles of the past 100 years.

We were too preoccupied with wildlife restoration and the pleasure of the hunt to keep a collective eye on where we came from. With the passage of a generation or two, it was easy for us to become focused on the present and what lay ahead. Little note was taken of Aldo Leopold's council: *"To think straight on recreational quality, an historical perspective is essential."* The consequence of this omission was a generation of wildlife managers educated by a system that generally avoided teaching conservation history or philosophy. Likewise forgotten was the observation of D'ing Darling: *"I'm learning one thing the hard way, and that is that you have to re-educate the public mind about every fifteen or twenty years or it forgets everything learned a while back."*

From a wildlife management perspective, however, the restoration of game species was spectacular and it had to happen first. The North American wildlife recovery is described well by Canadian wildlife biologist, Shane Mahoney. Philosophically shaped by his homeland, Newfoundlander Mahoney views the world from a relatively harsh physical environment. It is a place he simply describes as a rock sticking out of the North Atlantic. To survive there one either hunts on land or out on a stormy sea. Mahoney gave us a tidy summary of our achievement:

> We should engage in a continent wide explosion of congratulations to North America and the peoples who live here, for we have achieved what most of the world can only dream about...wildlife abundance in the midst of human population increases and enough fire power to destroy every living creature. Instead we have geese on our lawns, turkeys in our driveways, deer in our fields and bears in our apple trees!

Thus endowed, we began the 21st Century. The North American continent has been stocked with game and the hunt nurtured through a century, and then both the animals and the hunt passed to our custody. If the restoration of wildlife hadn't been a success, historical reflection on principles and our predecessors would have been little more than academic exercise. Because the movement was successful, however, we have the luxury of contemplating our course through another century. It will be a course navigated in a dynamic society where new values will take their own measure of traditional practices. We need to address our future with one eye firmly fixed on the same star our forefathers followed. It is a bright star fueled by the ideals that brought us to our new century. It bore an ethical code built on the principle of common ownership, conservation of the hunted, preservation of wild places, and always, *fair chase*. We hunters are not lost in an intellectual wilderness. The track that brought us to where we are is clear enough to follow.

Mahoney clearly articulated the most important principle embedded in our achievement.

> The North American conservation achievement is outstanding for many reasons....Unlike earlier historic movements in Africa, Asia and Europe, which were almost consistently tied to an exclusivity tradition, spurred by the caste notions...in Greek and Roman culture, by monarchist traditions of the Middle Ages, or by the aristocratic world views of the post-Renaissance and colonial periods, the 'in situ' emergence of our tradition was based explicitly on inclusivity. Wildlife and Access to it was to be in the public domain, by law. [1]

This contemporary assessment presents a tidy package summing up not only *what* hunters accomplished, but *why*. Both are remarkably consistent with the vision for hunting offered by Theodore Roosevelt one hundred years ago:

> ...to preserve game...for...all lovers of nature, and to give reasonable opportunities for the exercise of the skill of the hunter, whether he is or is not a man of means. [2]

A comfortable confidence comes from finding philosophical support for something you want to believe. In this case, it is the remarkable consistency of belief at the core of the North American conservation model—and why it worked. It worked because it was designed for all the people. The basic principle of *inclusion* comes to us from Theodore

Roosevelt—his vision forged well over a century ago while hunting on the North Dakota frontier. Then confirmation of the same principle, just as clearly articulated, by Shane Mahoney, a contemporary hunter and wildlife scientist living on a rock jutting out of the North Atlantic. What these contributors have in common is an attachment to nature and wisdom born of the hunt.

The wildlife abundance of our time demonstrates that we have the management skills and resources to meet our ethical responsibility to the animals we hunt. We have seen to the welfare of the animals. We understand and practice the biology of game production and conservation. The challenge now is to save 'the hunt' associated with the game animals and our place in nature. Hunting is as old as our humanity. It is a natural relationship basic to life on earth. This relationship has included human hunters on this continent for more than 15,000 years. Hunting—an activity that circumstance and tradition now require us to define as the 'fair chase' pursuit of free-ranging wildlife—is available to anyone capable of taking up the chase.

By themselves, those who whine about animal rights and rail against killing animals are not going to destroy hunting. An equally serious threat to hunting is brought to our threshold by a host of questionable 'fellow travelers' trying to crowd under the hunter's banner:

- Hunting is threatened by those who throw up high fences to make something private out of the public's wildlife and make captive animals out of what must remain wild.
- The hunt fades when participants are required to pay private fees to follow the track of a public resource.
- Domesticated wildlife spreading diseases into wild

populations is clearly a threat, as are baiting and feeding practices that spread the pathogens.
- The peril to hunting escalates as gadgets replace competence, and catered, quick kills replace patience and an honest relationship with nature.
- Rock bottom is reached when shooters buy captive animals so they can kill them to have a 'trophy'—and a lie—to hang on the wall.
- The ultimate mockery is the shooting of captive animals—promoted, advertised, and sold as a hunt. Roosevelt's vision of 'honor through effort' is ridiculed and shamed by genetically boosted, antler-stimulated, mutant, tamed trophies.
- Finally, the wild places where we go to become hunters continue to erode. This century's motorized contraptions, high-tech advantages, urban sprawl, and the mall all add to the toll.

These are our challenges and they must be addressed with the same vigor shown by the hunters who came before us. As biologist Mahoney put it, *"We cannot bleed and gut the most successful conservation strategy in the world on the altar of philosophies we honestly believe not in the best long term interest of nature conservation."*

Likewise, we must reject the argument that all forms of shooting animals—wild, semi-wild, and domestic—must be defended for the sake of hunter unity. Tolerance of the lowest ethical standards for the sake of unity simply demeans us all. We must travel the road of high principle and not compromise to the notion of 'circling the wagons' in hunting's defense. Retreats to fortresses have histories of defeat that have been true from the French defense of Dien Bien Phu back to the Alamo and beyond. We cannot will it otherwise. Mahoney put it well when he counseled, *"circling the wagons will lead only to a collapse to the center when what is needed is a determined ride to the hinterlands."* We would do well to remember that Davey Crockett died in the fall of the Alamo, while Sam Houston defeated Santa Anna on the open plains of San Jacinto.

Challenges to hunting are real. Honoring the principles of fair chase, maintaining the public-trust in wildlife management, and protecting our vanishing wild places will be difficult. However, they must be our agenda and we must engage the issues with intellectual energy and physical vigor. We cannot leave it to someone else. The question now is the same as it was in 1909. Are we capable of protecting the North American hunting heritage? Will we measure up to the expectation passed to us by history? Unlike Taft, we can learn from history and then be true to our heritage. We still have the chance to approach the grave overlooking Oyster Bay with a sense of honor for having lived up to the expectations of a giant. The alternative is too grim to contemplate. Like Taft, we too could be left to weep over a grave because we found reason to excuse ourselves from the expectations passed on to our hunter's camp.

The Taft story is important because it reveals our choices while we still have them. The principles followed by Roosevelt, A.A. Richardson, D'ing Darling, Aldo Leopold and thousands of others who saved wild North America are clearly visible. The illustrations of Darling are still alive. The veterans of San Juan Hill and the hunters who took TR to his final rest went up that slope with their sense of honor and pride whole. Their tears were neither bitter nor shed in shame. We must be as worthy.

Preparing the Future

For those of us in love with the outdoor experience, every day afield is an expression of expectation and hope. We are a hopeful lot and the most hopeful among us are our youth. They are the raw material of our future. The preparation of this human resource, our investment in the future, resides in hunter education programs. For more than half a century, North America's hunter education programs have been preparing and molding the future of hunting. It is probably the most under-funded and under-appreciated component of the North American hunting community.

Hunter education is an effort built with and sustained by thousands of volunteers. These faithful instructors prepare more than a half million new hunters for entry into our community each year. Three short stories will help us realize and appreciate the values, the promise, and the hope of the youth now flowing into our ranks every year.

A Story From Utah

In November of 2000, I found myself deep in the North American hinterlands traveling to the Dugway Research and Development Center in Utah's Great Basin Desert. Meeting space at the federal facilities had been reserved for a workshop with Utah's hunter education instructors. On the way from Salt Lake City, my host Lt. Lenny Rees of the Utah Division of Wildlife gave me a grand tour. It was a half-day trip that

Rifle in Hand

included watching bands of wild horses and visiting the preserved remnants of the Pony Express station at Simpson Springs. In a matter of hours we traveled from Pony Express and wild horses to a rocket-proving ground and e-mail. During such experiences a person's mind is forced to deal with the passage of time, things that change, and things that can never change.

During the conference lunch break, I was fortunate to sit across the table from Jay Potter, a Utah instructor, and his daughter Elizabeth. In the course of conversation I learned that Jay was an engineer who worked with rocket fuel. Both Jay and Elizabeth are active hunters and what they represent struck home as a clear example of the cultural value of our North American hunting heritage. Jay was preserving an incredible range of choices for his daughter and for all young people in our society.

Because we are a free people, any young person in our society can aspire to rocket into space exploration—riding the cutting edge of our technology. That same person can also choose to hunt and thereby engage in the most fundamental ritual of our humanity. A young person can also choose to do both. Today in North America the widest range of human experiences and choices is being nurtured and can be offered to any person to enrich their life. Our form of governance and our cultural development now holds that whole spectrum of choices, and we can offer them to our children—that's special.

Another Story From Iowa

In America's heartland, geography, topography and fecundity smile on Iowa. In the context of conservation history, the Iowa people smiled back. Iowa passed its first law

Rifle in Hand

to protect wildlife in 1857, a year before Theodore Roosevelt's birth. That law included a restriction on *"killing, trapping or ensnaring any deer, elk, fawn, wild turkey, prairie hen or chicken between February 1 and July 15 except on one's own property."* We know that 30 years later a young D'ing Darling saw buffalo hides being barged down the Missouri River near Sioux City, Iowa. That was also the same decade that marked the birth of Aldo Leopold in Burlington near Iowa's other big river, the Mississippi.

On June 9, 2000, I landed in Des Moines on my way to The Youth Hunter Education Challenge camp sponsored by Iowa State University (ISU) and the Iowa Department of Natural Resources (DNR). Organized by ISU Extension Wildlife Specialist Jim Pease, and Iowa's DNR hunter education coordinator Rod Slings, the camp was three days of field experience and classroom education. The wildlife program at ISU can trace its roots to 1932 when Darling was on the Iowa Fish and Game Commission. From this position he helped create and fund *"a cooperative program for research and wildlife conservation"* at the university. [1]

More than 100 young people ages 12 to 18 who had already completed a hunter education course were participating. The field events were structured to test their skills with rifle, shotgun, muzzleloader, bow, and compass. There were simulated hunting trails with situations calling for ethical and moral choices. In specially designed courses, the students encountered lost and wounded hunters as well as poachers. Wildlife identification and knowledge of hunting seasons were woven into the experience and testing. Every participant demonstrated his or her acquired ability to shoot, to think, to exercise value judgements, and to make ethical choices.

Rifle in Hand

Several of the events involved 'live fire.' In one particular event, each participant was accompanied to shooting positions by an instructor/mentor. A number of firing points were located along a ridgeline trail that led down through a heavy canopy of hardwood trees. To guide the student and ensure safety, each instructor/mentor placed his hand on the student's shoulder. Thus connected, they moved together through the forest to the firing points. The student moved with *rifle in hand*.

I watched this event through several rotations of students. As I did, the hand on the shoulder of the young person became spellbinding. I thought then, and think now, that in the hand of the instructor I also saw the hand of Roosevelt, the hand of Leopold, the hand of D'ing Darling. Each mentor's touch was the hand of passage. The connection was more than symbolic. The hunting heritage was passing to the next generation right before my eyes, and it was real.

The sight of these pairs of hunters passing down the trail through the hardwoods is imprinted deep in my mind. The more I learn about Theodore Roosevelt's legacy, the stronger the sight of his hand becomes. The vision of a young D'ing Darling romping through head-high grasslands, pausing as a barge of buffalo hides drifts down the Missouri River, melded seamlessly into the eager young faces passing down the trail. The thought of Aldo Leopold's 25-year conservation plan for Iowa blended smoothly into the landscape, embracing the whole event. Hunter education was melding the past with the future—and it too was special.

A Story From Wyoming

Wildlife has been a big part of life in Wyoming since the Verendryes expedition entered the Big Horn Mountains in 1743, 33 years before the Declaration of Independence. Wyoming's Jackson Hole country was prominent in the storied years of the mountain men and the beaver fur trade of the 1800s. Conservation was also important to Wyoming people, and in 1869 their first Territorial Legislature passed *"An Act for the Protection of Game and Fish in the Territory of Wyoming."* That was seven years before Colonel Custer died on the hills above the Little Big Horn River a little north of the Wyoming border. In 1873, the *Cheyenne Leader* reported an estimated 200,000 buffalo had been slaughtered the previous year.

Protection came early in Wyoming's history with the creation of Yellowstone National Park in 1872 and with subsequent actions that protected the last remnants of big game in the park. In time, protection was extended into Jackson Hole, a favored rendezvous area of the mountain men, with the creation of Grand Teton National Park. The National Elk Refuge at Jackson became part of the conservation process and quickly became a national treasure.

Jackson is not your typical western cow town. When personal income in Wyoming is measured, Teton County is usually ranked near the top of the list. This concentration of wildlife and money is so convenient that an anti-hunting animal rights group opened an office there.

In October 1997 a youth hunt for 70 elk was authorized as part of the management strategy for the National Elk Refuge. The anti-hunting group offered a $1,000 mountain bike to any person who *"turns his or her elk permit and hunting license in to The Fund For Animals' Jackson office, and promises not to hunt for the remainder of the season."* [2] Not a single person accepted.

Rifle in Hand

A number of young hunters were asked, *"What would it take for you to give up your elk permit?"* Jessica Jackson replied, *"A recording contract as a singer."* Mark Gilbertson said, *"Not a bicycle."* Emily Brumstead topped them all when she stated, *"A bison permit."* These young people and their associates are the poster youth of the North American hunting heritage. The attitude and understanding shown by these people is not an accident. They are a reflection of the values of their hunting mentors and the quality of the hunter education program that touched them.

In February 2002 *Field and Stream* published the results of its "Young Writers Contest." The challenge was to respond to the question, "How hunting/fishing has influenced my life." The writers were from all across the country and their reflections revealed a rich collection of values and sensitivities. Harrison Tome of Jackson, Wyoming, put it as follows: *"You can't call yourself an outdoorsman. I've become an outdoorsman and a good citizen by living according to rules and ethics taught to me by other hunters and fishermen."*

These young people are coming into the hunting community by the hundreds of thousands each year. The new hunters are better prepared to engage in the hunt today than at any time since the hunt passed from native societies to modern cultures. If these seeds of our future fall on fertile ground, hunting will enjoy a prosperous tomorrow. They must, however, find the opportunity to hunt and to honestly engage in the fair chase pursuit of game. America's youth are much too smart to be deceived. If we offer them diminished wildness, compromised ethical standards, fabricated killing experiences, a commercial oligarchy of hunting, and abandonment of the pure principles of TR himself, then they will vanish quicker than a spooked elk in dark timber. This flow of youthful human assets is our most valuable resource. Their expectations are our future. Thankfully, they are high.

Our future

We have hunted for as long as we have been. Within our society, however, we are a slowly fading portion of the population. In Montana, our minority is 24 percent of the state's population—and that is the highest hunter participation level in the United States. Nationwide when the 21st Century began, about 14.6 million of us took to the field to hunt, and about 42.2 million of us had hunted sometime in our lives. [3] Each year more than a half million young hunters enroll in hunter education as a requirement to obtain a hunting license. Still, it is critical that we find ways to introduce even more people to the significance and joys of hunting.

I nurture a belief that people, eventually saturated and bored with electronic and artificial mind occupation, will seek a connection with nature and their place in it. A return to nature cycles through the human species, and nothing is more real, honest, and natural than the hunt. The reasons for this call to the hunt are buried in the tangled genetic protein of all the earth's progeny. From microbes to lions we are all either hunter or hunted. It was our past for several thousand generations and there is little reason to think it lost.

As hunters, it is up to us to prepare an invitation to other North Americans—an invitation that says 'come back to us and come back with us.' Let us take you to the absolute quiet of falling snow in heavy timber. Let us introduce you to the rush of a cackling pheasant erupting from possibility into reality. Wait with us among the autumn hardwoods to listen for the whitetail's rustling steps on fallen leaves. Let us

Rifle in Hand

help you send the sound of an elk's bugle into the forest when the aspen shimmer golden. Let us introduce you to a long dormant humility when the cougar screams in the darkness. Stand with us on the pre-dawn prairie long after the moon has set and the sky bursts with all the cosmic energy your senses can handle.

Let us take you beyond pavement and then beyond trail to places where every sight, scent, and sound comes from something absolutely wild. Let nature show you a new level of alertness, then let her hone that new awareness to an edge so real it will cut. There will be blood, and that too will be real. Then, when darkness comes again, let us watch the campfire's reflection dance with the excitement in your eyes as we listen to your tale of the hunt.

Epilogue

A lot of years have passed since my moose hunt in Montana's Elkhorn Mountains. The modest antlers hang patiently in an honored spot. When I pursued that young bull through the snowy mountains I knew nothing of TR's legacy, A.A. Richardson's courageous persistence, D'ing Darling's bold leadership, or Aldo Leopold's thoughtful insights. When I stalked that wild, meandering moose it did not occur to me that I was the grandson of a Lithuanian peasant exercising an American liberty, a liberty born of our rebellion. When I killed that moose my excitement and satisfaction were complete although my knowledge of the whole story was missing. I believe my contentment came because my engagement with the moose was fair and I hunted naturally with the heart of a hunter. Today, 30 years after that hunt, those moose antlers have become a treasure beyond measure, a treasure because I finally have learned why they are with me. I know whose hand rested on my shoulder when I slipped into the cold mountain forest—and it embraced me.

In these pages we have followed a well-marked trail through a little more than a century, examining how the hunt came to our time and who some of the heroes were. While history is perhaps interesting, the question is, can these thoughts, stories and words still impact us after a century? Can we still connect to the spirit of Theodore Roosevelt and find inspiration strong enough to apply to our lives?

Rifle in Hand

The answers are yes! Since the American tragedy of September 11, 2001, the name Todd Beamer has become synonymous with heroism. Todd was one of the leaders that thwarted the terrorist plot to turn a hijacked airplane, United Airlines Flight 93, into a flying bomb. It might have been aimed at our nation's capital. Beamer's last message, routed to an Airfone operator in Chicago, carried the story of the passengers' intent to take control of the plane. It was a heroic act and it was accomplished. The story, carried in the December 3, 2001, issue of *Newsweek*, included a passage about Todd's wife, Lisa, sorting through items in his den. The article included the following:

> It was on his desk that she found, on a folded piece of paper at the bottom of his in-box, a passage quoting Teddy Roosevelt: 'The credit belongs to the man who is actually in the arena…(whose) place shall never be with those cold and timid souls who know neither victory nor defeat.

Another *Newsweek* story, carried on January 14, 2002, covered the American Special Forces on the ground in Afghanistan. It included this passage:

> Green Berets like to say that their training—physically brutal as it is—favors brains over brawn. Team leader Dean quotes Shakespeare from memory. Mike, the weapons expert, keeps Teddy Roosevelt's passage about men who fight "in the arena" in his diary.

Rifle in Hand

The Theodore Roosevelt quote hangs framed on my wall and perhaps on yours. There is still a strong bond between Americans and their 26th President, the most popular person ever to hold our highest office. His popularity then and now was linked directly to his genuine fondness for the common American. As our President, he and his family were honored and literally showered with gifts from royalty around the world. In his time more than a few kings still occupied thrones in the civilized world. The Roosevelt family also received many material things from the industrial plutocracy that was forming in 20th Century America. Yet when writing his autobiography, TR addressed what he and his wife most valued:

> Perhaps our most cherished possessions are a Remington bronze, 'The Bronco Buster,' given by my men when the regiment was mustered out, and a big Tiffany silver vase given to Mrs. Roosevelt by the enlisted men of the battleship Louisiana….[1]

They were gifts from the common American people.
　　Later in life Roosevelt was commiserating with an old friend who suggested that the wilderness of the West would be the greatest memorial to his farsightedness. His response was, *"Bully, I had rather have it than a hundred stone monuments."*[2] In the end the American people had his likeness chiseled into the granite of Mount Rushmore, and TR got both.
　　Sadly, we no longer have such giants walking among us. Since there is not likely to be another Theodore Roosevelt in our time, perhaps we can find a touch of his spirit in each one of us. We can learn from the life he lived and the lessons

he left in his passing. We, North America's hunters, can and should stay connected to nature, take care of the wildness and wild things of earth, and nurture the hunt. We can do these things just as he did—*rifle in hand.*

> *"The things accomplished that have been enumerated above were of immediate consequence to the economic well-being of our people. In addition certain things were done of which the economic bearing was remote, but which bore directly upon our welfare, because they add to the beauty of living and therefore to the joy of life."*
>
> THEODORE ROOSEVELT,
> COMMENTING ON HIS CONSERVATION RECORD[3]

End Notes

Introduction

1 Stephen Ambrose, *Thomas Jefferson and Theodore Roosevelt, Theodore Roosevelt Association Journal*, Vol. XXX. #3, 2003.

The Train From Lithuania

1. MicroEncarta, Encart: Microsoft Coporation, 1997.
2. Edmund Morris, *Theodore Rex,* Random House, New York, 22001.
3. Paul Schullery, *Theodore Roosevelt: Wilderness Writings,* Gibbs M. Smith, Inc., Peregrine Smith books, Salt Lake City, Utah, 1986.
4. Ibid.

Last of the Buffalo Hunters

1. Larry Jahn, *A Look Behind, A look Ahead, Wyoming Wildlife,* January, 2000.
2. Nathan Miller, *Theodore Roosevelt A Life,* Quill William Morrow and Company, New York, 1992.
3. Joe Kosack, The Pennsylvanian Game Commission 1895-1995; 100 years of Conservation, Pennsylvania Game Commission, Harrisburg, PA, 1995.
4. John F. Organ and Eric K. Fritzell, *Trends in consumptive Recreation and the Wildlife Profession, Wild Society Bulletin,* Vol. 28, No. 4, Winter 2000.
5. Paul Russell Cutright, *Theodore Roosevelt the Naturalist,* Harper & Brothers, New York, 1956.
6. Harold and Irene Picton, *The Saga of the Sun,* Montana Department of Fish and Game, Helena, Montana, 1975.
7. Nathan Miller, Op. Cit.
8. Nathan Miller, Op. Cit.
9. Nathan Miller, Op. Cit.
10. Nathan Miller, Op. Cit.
11. Nathan Miller, Op. Cit.
12. John Reiger, *American Sportsmen and the Origins of Conservation,* Third, Revised and Expanded Edition, Oregon State University Press, Corvallis, OR, 2001.

The Conservation Idea

1. Peter Wild, *Pioneer Conservationists of Eastern America,* Mountain Press Publishing Missoula, MT, 1986.
2. Leonard H. Wurman, *Profile, George Bird Grinnell (1849-1938), Fair Chase, Fall 2002,* The Boone and Crockett Club, Missoula, MT.
3. Martin vs. Waddell 41 U.S. 367.
4. Susan Horner, *Embryo Not Fossil: Breathing Life Into the Public Trust in Wildlife,* University of Wyoming Land & Water Review, Vol. XXXV No. 1, Laramie, WY 2000.
5. Peter Wild, Op. Cit.
6. Leonard H. Wurman, Op. Cit.
7. Peter Wild, Op.Cit.
8. Theodore Roosevelt, *Theodore Roosevelt, An Autobiography,* DaCapo Press Inc., reprint, 1985.
9. Ibid.
10. Gifford Pinchot, *Breaking New Ground,* Island Press, Washington, D.C., 1998.

Taking Action

1. Donald Day, *The Hunting and Exploring Adventures of Theodore Roosevelt: Told in His own Words,* The Dial Press, New York, 1955.
2. Ibid.
3. Ibid.
4. John Reiger, Op.Cit.
5. John Organ, personal communication, November 5, 2003.
6. John Elliot, *T.R.'s Wilderness Legacy, National Geographic,* Vol.162 No. 3, September, 1982.
7. James Trefethen, *An American Crusade for Wildlife,* The Boone and Crockett Club, Alexandria, VA, 1975.
8. Paul Schullery, Op. Cit.
9. Paul Schullery, Op. Cit.
10. Peter Wild, Op. Cit.
11. Paul Schullery, Op. Cit.
12. Theodore Roosevelt, Op. Cit.
13. Geist, V., S. P.Mahoney, and J.F. Organ, *Why Hunting has Defined the North American Model of Wildlife Conservation, Transaction North American Wildlife and Natural Resource Conference. 66:175-185, 2001.*
14. Great Falls Tribune, *Marines Feast on Gazelles From Saddam's Preserve,* April 19, 2003 (page 3A).

Rifle in Hand

The Great Occasions

1. Nathan Miller, Op. Cit.
2. Public Broadcast System, *The President's Series, Theodore Roosevelt,* Turner Home Entertainment Inc., 1997.
3. Theodore Roosevelt, Op. Cit.
4. Jim Casada, *The Prodigal Years, South Carolina Wildlife,* Vol. 37, No., 1, January/February 1990. (All quotes from the A.A. Richardson story taken from this source.)
5. David Lendt, *The Life of Jay Norwood Darling,* The Maecenas Press, Mt. Pleasant, S.C., in cooperation with the J.N "Ding" Darling Foundatin Key Biscayne, FL, 2001.
6. Ibid.
7. Ibid.
8. Ibid.
9. Ibid.
10. Ibid.
11. Ibid.
12. Peter Wild, Op.Cit.
13. Aldo Leopold, *Origin and Ideal of Wilderness Areas, The Living Wilderness,* The Wilderness Society, July, 1940.
14. Dennis Roth, *The National Forests and the Campaign for Wilderness, Journal of Forest History,* July, 1985.
15. Aldo Leopold, *The Last Stand of the Wilderness, American Forests and Forest Life,* October, 1925.
16. Aldo Leopold, *Wilderness Values, The Living Wilderness,* The Wilderness Society, March, 1942.
17. John Reiger, Op. Cit.

Taft, Peril and Postcrity

1. John Morton Blum, *The Republican Roosevelt*, Harvard University Press,Cambridge, Massachusetts & London England, 1977.
2. Nathan Miller, Op. Cit.
3. Ibid.
4. Ibid.
5. Theodore Roosevelt, Op. Cit.
6. Nathan Miller, Op. Cit.
7. Ibid.

The Hunt that Must Survive

1. Shane Mahoney, *Wildlife Conservation in the 21st Century: Can Hunters and Anglers Continue to Lead?* 78th Annual Conference, Western Association of fish and Wildlife Agencies, Jackson, WY, 1998.
2. Paul Schullery, Op. Cit.

Preparing the Future

1. David L. Lendt, Op. Cit.
2. Jackson Hole News, Wednesday, October 8, 1997.
3. 2001 National Survey of Fishing, Hunting and Wildlife-Associated Recreation, USDI Fish and Wildlife Service, January 2003.

Epilogue

1. Theodore Roosevelt, Op.Cit.
2. Elliot, Op.Cit.
3. Theodore Roosevelt, Op.Cit.